D1255235

STUDIES IN ROMANCE LANGUAGES: 19

Julien Green
par
Denise de Bravura
-1954-

THE METAMORPHOSES OF THE SELF

The Mystic, the Sensualist, and the Artist in the Works of Julien Green

John M. Dunaway

THE UNIVERSITY PRESS OF KENTUCKY

Dunaway, John M 1945-
The metamorphoses of the self.

(Studies in romance languages ; 19)
Bibliography: p.
Includes index.
1. Green, Julien, 1900- —Criticism and interpretation. I. Title. II. Series.
PQ2613.R3Z64 843'.9'12 78-88007
ISBN 0-8131-1364-4

Scholarly publisher for the Commonwealth,
serving Berea College, Centre College of Kentucky,
Eastern Kentucky University, The Filson Club,
Georgetown College, Kentucky Historical Society,
Kentucky State University, Morehead State University,
Murray State University, Northern Kentucky University,
Transylvania University, University of Kentucky,
University of Louisville, and Western Kentucky University.

Editorial and Sales Offices: Lexington, Kentucky 40506

For Michel . . .

il mio autore

Contents

Acknowledgments

I would like to thank the Duke University Graduate School for the dissertation travel grant that enabled me to begin this study in Paris, and the Mercer University Committee on Faculty Research Grants for generously subsidizing publication costs.

Chapter Six is reprinted with permission of the *South Atlantic Bulletin*, in which it appeared in slightly altered form.

I am especially grateful to Wallace Fowlie for his guidance and friendship throughout this project. I thank Mme Eveline Garnier and M. Michel Guiomar, who helped me crystallize the first ideas I began to have on Green and made me feel like a writer.

I was particularly fortunate to be granted an interview with M. Green, and his offer to read this study gave it added significance for me. Green and the Librairie Plon have graciously granted permission to reprint the portrait by Denise de Bravura which serves as frontispiece.

Finally, my warmest thanks go to my wife Trish, who not only taught me to rewrite but above all gave me the feeling that she always believed in me.

Abbreviations

The following abbreviations and shortened forms are used in textual references to the works of Julien Green:

AS: *L'Autre sommeil*

J: *Journal*

MCO: *Mille chemins ouverts*

Min: *Minuit*

PAJ: *Partir avant le jour*

TL: *Terre lointaine*

Vis: *Le Visionnaire*

Voy: *Le Voyageur sur la terre*

Introduction

The warm reception that greeted the publication of Julien Green's latest novel, *L'Autre*, in February of 1971 signaled the beginning of a year of unaccustomed notoriety for this often neglected figure in contemporary French letters. By April the press was alive with talk of Julien Green for the French Academy. The problem was that Green was an American citizen, a status that he would automatically forfeit if he were to request French citizenship. The Academy submitted the problem to President Pompidou, who declared Green to be already, in effect, a French citizen by virtue of his contributions to the literature of France and his service in the French Army in 1918-1919. On June 3, 1971, an overwhelming majority of the Academy voted for Julien Green to occupy, appropriately enough, the chair vacated by his longtime friend François Mauriac, whose death in the fall of 1970 was the occasion of national mourning and whose funeral eulogy was delivered by Green himself.

Who is this Julien Green, first foreigner ever to be elected to the French Academy? One might expect such a question in this country: Green is not widely known in the United States. The question, however, needs a surprising amount of illumination in the very country where Green makes his home. For example, Robert de Saint-Jean reports that André Gide was never quite able to understand his young friend's origin. He persisted in thinking that he must have been born in some French-speaking part of North America. Green succeeded in convincing him that he was not born in Canada, but Gide died with the mistaken notion that Green was a native of New Orleans.[1] More recently, *Le Monde*'s special feature on the occasion of Green's election to the Academy included a biographical sketch that confused his father's home state with his mother's.[2]

The often confused facts of Julien Green's origin are that he was born in Paris on September 6, 1900. His parents were both American citizens, Edward Moon Green being a native Virginian and Mary Hartridge Green, a Georgian. The family (Julien was the youngest of eight children) had moved to France in 1895 when Edward Green was appointed European agent for the Southern Cotton Seed Oil Company. Thus, Julien Green enjoys the unique status among his colleagues in the Academy of being at once a native Parisian, an American citizen by birth, and now a French citizen by order of the president of the Republic.

Young Julien[3] grew up speaking French and acquired English only through the persistence of his mother, who was determined not to permit his original nationality to be obscured by the family's newly adopted country. Green's parents, especially his mother, were quite proud of their Southern heritage and passed on to him a deep love for the traditions of the Old South. Mrs. Green's home town of Savannah became an inaccessible dreamland in young Julien's mind, and the Confederate States were a symbol of a remote and beckoning utopia with all the charms of a *pays lointain*. As we shall see more clearly in examining his autobiography, Green's parents also passed on to him a puritanical religious heritage that became the source of both shattering anxieties and much of his literary production.

Except for a brief residence near Saint-Germain-en-Laye, the Greens lived in Paris throughout Julien's youth, mostly in the Passy district. Julien was educated at the well-known *lycée* Janson-de-Sailly. His childhood was a lyrically happy one, but it was a fragile kind of happiness whose fabric had begun to erode by the end of 1914. The shock of the Great War undermined the weak health of Mary Hartridge Green, and her death in December of that year left an irreparable void in Julien's life. Julien and his father converted to Catholicism in 1915, and by the time he attained his *baccalauréat* he had announced his decision to prepare himself to join a monastic order. Throughout his military service and most of his college years, the monastic vocation was the estate to which he aspired.

In 1917, Green joined the American Field Service as an ambulance driver and later served in the same capacity with the American Red Cross. In 1918, he joined the Foreign Legion in order to be transferred into the French Artillery as an *aspirant*. After finishing artillery school, he was assigned to occupational duty in the Rhineland. Upon demobilization in 1919, Green learned that his Uncle Walter Hartridge of Savannah was offering to send him to the University of Virginia for four years. Green accepted and came to Charlottesville, Virginia, in 1919, his first visit to the land of his origins. Instead of the childhood dream of an antebellum utopia, however, Green found the South growing out of its Reconstruction mentality into a modern and very alien culture. His longing for the familiar sights of Paris made him a quiet, melancholy student who seemed aloof to many of his classmates. But almost unconsciously, Julien was being captivated by the charms of the Old South that survived as vestiges of the land his mother had so deeply loved. Moreover, the young man was finally beginning to acknowledge his homosexual nature during his years at Virginia. Some of his best works of fiction would later be set in what Green's imagination recreated as "le Sud."

Since returning to Paris from Virginia in 1922, Green has lived there continuously except for three visits to the United States in the 1930s and the duration of World War II, which he also spent in this country. Besides serving a short term of duty with the United States Army, he spent the war years working for the Office of War Information in New York, teaching and lecturing at numerous colleges, and writing his only book in English, *Memories of Happy Days*.

The trauma of discovering his homosexuality led to a long separation from the Church, but in 1939 Green was "reconverted" and has been a devout Catholic since. His literary production is imposing in scope and is still growing: twelve novels, five short stories or *nouvelles*, three plays, a four-volume autobiography, the *Journal* (1928 to present), and numerous essays and translations.

Julien Green now lives in a quiet apartment on the rue Vaneau with his sister Anne, a novelist in her own right and the translator of many of her brother's books into English. Having kept himself accessible to his readers, Green readily accepts visits from those who are seriously interested in his work, but he is a compulsive writer and remains faithful to Baudelaire's regimen of "le travail quotidien."

The works of Julien Green bear witness to a perpetual inner struggle based on a duality that is fundamental to his psychological makeup. He says in the *Journal* that he can understand only two types of human personalities: the mystic and the sensualist. These are precisely the two selves that are at odds in Green's inner struggle, a kind of "Spleen et Idéal" conflict that recalls Baudelaire's statement in *Mon coeur mis à nu:* "Il y a dans tout homme, à toute heure, deux postulations simultanées, l'une vers Dieu, l'autre vers Satan."[4] In all of his writing, Green is constantly addressing himself to "le problème des deux réalités" (J, 636),[5] the carnal reality versus the metaphysical reality, and seeking his own place in the tension between the two forces. With the mystical and erotic selves constantly struggling for ascendency, the initial reaction is a desire for escape and a refusal to accept reality on such difficult terms. But the eventual result is the affirmation of a third self that resolves the first two at a deeper level of meaning.

This study seeks to examine the identity of Julien Green within the context of his literary production. Various labels have been attached to Green in an effort to characterize cogently for the public the nature of his writing. The most persistent epithet has been that of the Catholic writer, and one of the purposes of this study is to demonstrate the reasons for the inadequacy of such a label. The aspect of Green's writing that is most neglected in the Catholic interpretation is the strong erotic element that conflicts so violently with the spiritual aspirations of his protagonists. The struggle of these two forces is the basic opposition of the first two Greenian selves, the mystic and the sensualist. The fact that the erotic dimension of Green's writing is often homosexual intensifies the violence of the inner struggle when one considers his puritanical background.

This study is not intended to prove that Green is essentially a homosexual writer. It does seek to demonstrate that the importance of homosexuality, and the erotic element in general, makes it misleading to refer to Green as a Catholic writer. The level on which Green's fiction treats homosexuality preserves the solemn dignity of the subject in the same sense that Racine preserved the solemn dignity of incestuous passion in *Phèdre*. Nevertheless, it must be remembered that sexuality in all its manifestations was regarded as impure by the young Julien Green. And because of his puritanical background, sexual inversion has always carried a moral stigma for him. This study seeks further to show what aspects of Green's writing gave rise to the persistent Catholic label and what aspects, on the other hand, led to the gradual tendency in Greenian criticism to admit the importance of erotic aspects of his fictional and nonfictional works.

It is only natural that misleading images of this writer should have arisen. One of the peculiar aspects of his writing is the process of *dédoublement* that so many of his characters experience. Daniel O'Donovan in *Le Voyageur sur la terre*, for example, has a companion and guide whom we eventually discover to be an imaginary projection of a particular aspect of his own personality. Indeed, the very act of writing for Julien Green is an attempt to resolve a profoundly divided self and to reach new depths of self-discovery. Especially in the world of Green's fiction, the amorphous, bewildering metamorphoses of the self are intimately involved in the drama of each protagonist. Ultimately, they lead to a personal myth, a heroic version of the visionary artist which is the most profound identity to which a writer may aspire.

The critical attention that has been accorded Julien Green thus far is lamentably inadequate, considering the prominent position among contemporary French writers that he has now attained. The bulk of what has been written on him tends to oversimplify the task of critical analysis and has contributed greatly to the most common misconception of Green, the myth of the Catholic writer. The label has plagued Green since 1927, when the original edition of *Adrienne Mesurat* was published in the *Roseau d'or* series, directed by Jacques Maritain. Green was naturally classified among the other contributors in the series, alongside such names as Henri Ghéon, Jacques Rivière, and Stanislas Fumet.

Green himself expressed displeasure with the Catholic label very early in his career. Like Mauriac, he could not let his religion affect the purity of his art. "Quand même je serais catholique, il me semble que ce titre de romancier catholique me ferait toujours horreur" (J, 10).[6] Paradoxically, Green's own *Journal* has contributed considerably to the very label that he has tried to avoid, for the typically Greenian duality of spirit and flesh is portrayed in the *Journal* from a markedly spiritual point of view. It might be observed in this connection that the critics who emphasize Green's mystical self make extensive use of the *Journal* as a source. Father Charles Moëller's interpretation, for example, is at bottom an evaluation of Green the man rather than a critical analysis of Green the writer.[7]

Aside from the spiritual dimension of Green's work, early critics were impressed most often by the nightmarish atmosphere in which his novels took place. The sinister quality of the supernatural and the morbidity of exterior reality in Green's fiction led many to compare him to the Brontë sisters and to Hawthorne and Poe. André Rousseaux's phrase, *réalisme magique,* well describes the emphasis of what little critical attention was devoted to Green before 1940. His early fiction is indeed characterized by the hallucinatory atmosphere that struck his first critics, but there is little attempt on their part to delve into the deeper psychological situation that created such an atmosphere.

All of the critical material written on Julien Green before 1963 lacks the understanding of the young Green's sexual drama that only his autobiography gives.[8] After this momentous confession, the myth of Green as the Catholic writer could no longer hold sway. The erotic elements, often latent in earlier works and increasingly autobiographical in later ones, could no longer be ignored. The basic duality of spiritual fervor and sexual desire had to be acknowledged. Surprisingly, many of the books on Green that have appeared since 1963 take little note of the autobiography. But the acknowledgment of the importance of sexuality—especially sexual inversion—has become more and more common.[9]

The majority of those who have written about Julien Green will agree that the basic tension on which all his works are structured lies in the duality of the spiritual and the carnal. What none of them has yet established is the resolution of this duality in Green's art. The identity quest is one of the most powerful motives of his works. The Greenian hero, bewildered by the *dédoublement* of his self-image, seeks his destiny in the ambivalence of spiritual and erotic realities. Through the metamorphoses of the self his deepest aspiration is "dire sa vérité." Each in his own darkness (*Chaque homme dans sa nuit*) advances toward the light of his destined identity only by means of the visionary reality which is the medium of the artist, the third self.

In this study, I shall begin with an examination of the autobiographical context of Julien Green's works, in which the duality of mystic and sensualist is quite clearly polarized. I shall then proceed through a selected series of his fictional works in an attempt to show the birth and nature of the third self as a personal myth of the artist. I shall consider the fiction in chronological order with the intention of demonstrating the evolution of the myth of the third self in Green's career.

Chapter One

Journal and Autobiography: The First Two Selves

The *Journal* of Julien Green is a work of widely diversified themes. It records Green's personal impressions of the important literary figures he has known: Mauriac, Malraux, Bernanos, Cocteau, and especially Maritain and Gide. One also finds the author's reactions to his voluminous reading, which ranges from esoteric religious writings of the seventeenth and eighteenth centuries to American and English novelists of the nineteenth century. Among his *livres de chevet* must be included the Bible, Pascal, Péguy, Keats, Baudelaire. The author touches on music, as well as important ideas on esthetics and the relationship between art and morality. But the dominant theme throughout the *Journal* is the spiritual odyssey of a soul struggling with the problems of the flesh. "J'ai désiré trop de choses, à la fois la chair et l'esprit. . . . J'ai essayé de retrouver un équilibre de plus en plus menacé par la dualité de ma nature" (J, 171, 540).

Clearly, the fundamental tension of spiritual and erotic realities is all-important throughout the *Journal*. Green has experienced bitter suffering because of the simple fact of possessing a body. There is a kind of inferno of desire within him that is never extinguished, and at the same time a desperate thirst after the things of the spirit. In the *Journal*, the spiritual aspect of this polarity is by far the predominant one.

Volume I of the journal begins in 1928, during Green's extended separation from the Catholic Church. The first part of the *Journal*, then, was written in the most erotically oriented and spiritually alienated moment of his life. In 1930, for example, he referred in *L'Autre sommeil* to "la superstition catholique" (AS, 168) and made other allusions that indicate alienation from the Church. It was at this time in Green's career that André Gide's influence was of major importance for him. Gide was the universally acclaimed artist whose attentions to the young Green were quite flattering. He made light jest of the vanguard of Catholic writers who were trying to win him to the Church, and Green, who was the object of the same kind of pressure, was clearly on Gide's side. After Green's reconversion in 1939 and his return to Paris after the war, Gide never tired of trying to convince Green that he had no place among the Catholics.

In spite of Green's anti-Catholicism at the beginning of the *Journal*, the entries of the 1930s began to reveal a slow spiritual development that would culminate in his reconversion to Catholicism in 1939. On one hand, a religious conversion at that stage of his life seemed only a means of escaping from his moral problems. His Puritan's conscience told him that sexual inversion rendered him unworthy of calling himself Christian. The radical commitment to Christ's teachings that he required of the French Catholics in his fiery "Pamphlet" of 1924 was the same that he expected of himself, if he was to reconvert. There were also moments, however, at which he was dimly aware that his truancy from the Church would not last.

Relu des pages de ce journal de 1928 à 1935. Je crois que dans le cahier que j'achève en ce moment, on verra les indices d'un changement intérieur, bien que les circonstances de ma vie extérieure restent les mêmes. [J, 191]

One of the most arresting aspects of Green's *Journal* is the prominence of what must be called mystical experiences. They occur without warning and are like "un subit retour de toute mon enfance" (J, 122-23). These privileged moments, which appear also in the autobiography and the fiction, are given much attention, as we might expect, in Georges Poulet's chapter on Green. According to Poulet, the suspension of time and movement in these experiences accomplishes "le remplacement du temps humain par une tranquillité que ne trouble aucun souci temporel."[1]

It is impossible to spend an hour's tête-à-tête with M. Green without sensing this "other reality" that emanates from the inner life of the man. The atmosphere created by the following passages from the *Journal* is very much the same atmosphere evoked by private conversation with him.

Cet étrange moment de bonheur que rien n'explique. . . . Il y a des moments où il fond sur nous, sans raison apparente. . . . On se sent tout à coup absurdement heureux . . . si heureux qu'on voudrait mourir, afin de prolonger à l'infini ce moment extraordinaire. [J, 114-15]

Avant-hier en traversant la rue du Bac, j'ai éprouvé pendant une ou deux secondes, pas plus, cette indescriptible sensation de bonheur dont j'ai parlé. Le monde s'est aboli autour de moi et avec le monde, le temps, ce cauchemar. Je me demande quelquefois si ce n'est pas là comme un avant-goût de la vie éternelle, une sorte d'irruption de l'éternité dans le temps. [J, 285]

The nostalgia for sainthood is one of the more poignant motifs in Green's diary. As an adolescent, his spiritual aspirations were irrepressible. Recalling the time when he wanted to become a religious, he makes it clear that that ambition had an indelible mark on the rest of his life.

J'aurais voulu être un saint. C'est tout. Je ne puis rien ajouter à cette parole. Une grande partie de ma vie ne me ressemble pas. Je sens vivement que je passe sans cesse à côté de celui que j'aurais voulu être, et d'une certaine manière, il existe, il est là et il est triste, et sa tristesse est la mienne. [J, 285]

He recalls his summers in Savannah (1920 and 1921), which were marked by "crises de piété" (J, 4). He fancied himself transported to his own Thebaid where he would enjoy the bizarre happiness of the ascetic hermit, an image that recalls Flaubert's *Tentation de Saint Antoine*, with which Green was well acquainted.[2] He describes the "drames de conscience" of his fifteenth year, when he inscribed his sins on the wall of his room. He was in love with God, with the Church, and with "tout un monde invisible" which held an irresistible attraction for him.

What had intervened between the aspirations of the adolescent and the Julien Green of the 1930s, who was desperately seeking relief from his anxieties and obsessions? The ecstatic dreams of his adolescence had been utterly shattered by his first carnal sins, as he calls them, which brought about "une connaissance plus profonde de moi-même" (J, 104). At the same time, the gradual evolution from the period of doubt brought on by his loss of innocence to the reconversion of 1939 is, in a sense, the plot of the early part of the *Journal*. It was a kind of truancy period in which Green strayed far from the Church but never lost his faith in God. "L'idée que Dieu pût ne pas être ne m'a jamais seulement effleuré" (J, 316).

In 1932 he explained that he hesitated to speak of religion because there lay in him "un fanatique mal assoupi que je tiens à ne pas réveiller" (J, 62). That fanatic could be called Théophile Delaporte,. the pseudonym under which Green wrote his first work to be published in France, the "Pamphlet contre les Catholiques de France" (1924). The "Pamphlet" reveals the reformer's zeal of a Calvin, preaching the doctrine of hell and the damnation of all but the few elect. Yet, it was written in the midst of Green's estrangement from religion.

The indications of Green's return to Catholicism were increasingly evident during the 1930s. In spite of a professed inability to pray after 1928, he insisted in the spring of 1934 that "dans le fond de mon coeur il y a encore la foi" (J, 160), and less than two weeks later, suddenly stricken with "l'angoisse," he found himself fervidly praying in the Virgin's chapel of Saint-Sulpice. In the fall of the same year he wrote: "Je me suis laissé séduire par le monde créé, mais il y a en moi des éléments de résistance" (J, 178).

Two significant developments of the 1930s were Green's decision to learn Hebrew in order to study the Scriptures more profitably and his growing interest in Buddhism, whose influence was evident in *Minuit* (1936). He stated that Buddhism had helped him overcome his obsessive fear of death. Much has been made of the importance of Oriental religions in this period,[3] and Green admits that the first part of *Varouna* (1940) was written while he still believed in metempsychosis. The intensity of his spiritual quest is reflected in the frequent discussion of mystical writings which interested him during this period: Saint John of the Cross, *Imitatio Christi*, Saint Theresa of Avila, for example. On January 29, 1939, Green included a significantly elliptical entry: "D'une pénible crise religieuse que j'ai traversée ce mois-ci il ne reste que quelques notes éparses dans mes petits carnets rouges. J'ai été horriblement secoué" (J, 309). It was the last reference to the spiritual crisis before the year's interruption in the *Journal* caused by the outbreak of hostilities that became World War II.

When the *Journal* resumed in July of 1940, there was an unmistakably new tone in the book. The term quietude could never be applied to Julien Green. Indeed, the tragic events in France that had forced him to live in "exile" during the war left him little security, and his erotic obsessions were never silenced. It is obvious, however, that after 1939 Green had a new source of strength on which he had been unable to rely before the war. The entry of February 28, 1941, offers an important account of the events of April 1939. In the midst of the influence of the Hindu mystics, Green happened upon a short treatise on Purgatory written by Saint Catherine of Genoa which had a profound effect on his thinking. A conversation with Maritain led him to discredit the Hindu mystics' ideas on metempsychosis. Green stated that his reconversion was "le résultat de ces faits, ainsi que d'autres d'un caractère plus secret'' (J, 379). In the last part of *Varouna*, which he had begun under the influence of Oriental religion, he tried to ''lessiver la métempsychose dans les eaux du baptême'' (J, 379).

From 1939 to the present, Julien Green has remained faithful to the Catholic Church. There have been moments of devastating anxiety and depression that are obliquely referred to in the *Journal*. ''Ces journées affreusement mémorables. . . . La crise religieuse que je traverse a commencé le 30 juin. Je me demande jusqu'où l'on peut aller sans perdre la raison'' (J, 718). But the overall impression created by the *Journal* is one of a man of extraordinary spiritual strength. He stated in 1955 that ''depuis 1938, je n'ai jamais eu l'ombre d'un doute, en ce qui concerne la foi'' (J, 1021). And less than a year before that statement he wrote that since the age of fifteen he had never felt so close to or in such perfect accord with the Church.

The image of Green the mystic is greatly enhanced in the *Journal* by his emphasis on the importance of the Bible. Daily reading of the Holy Scriptures was a family ritual instituted by Mrs. Green that her son has continued since his childhood. In his most trying moments the Bible was the refuge to which Green most often turned. There are numerous passages in the *Journal* similar to the following: ''longue lecture de la Bible pour essayer de tout remettre en place'' (J, 849). Green has attempted to give some idea of the immense importance of the Scriptures in his life.

> Il y a des moments—je ne le dis pas sans hésitation—où je repousse la tentation d'ouvrir la Bible, parce que je sais toute la force d'envoûtement de ce livre. C'est beaucoup plus qu'un livre, pour moi, c'est une voix et une personne. [J, 731]

The allusions to the problems of the sensualist in the diary, on the other hand, are sketchy: ''J'ai par moments une révolte contre le plaisir, contre la place qu'il tient dans ma vie. . . . Ce matin, en révolte contre le plaisir dont je ne vois pas comment on se passerait'' (J, 56, 65). There are references to the erotic obsessions, but only in vague terms such as ''le plaisir . . . le désir . . . la chair.'' The problem never receives explicit development, and the homosexual aspect is hardly even mentioned. In fact, the diary's reticence concerning Green's psychoerotic dilemma has tended to perpetuate the myth of the Catholic writer. Green is aware of this problem himself.

Si l'on découvrait ce journal, il donnerait de moi une idée fort inexacte, car je n'y mets guère que ma vie extérieure; ce qui se passe en moi, et qui est en contradiction absolue avec ma vie extérieure, je ne puis en parler, ou j'en parle très mal. [J, 231]

He realizes that the *Journal* treats all too superficially the incessant struggle within him between the spirit and the flesh.

When Green began his *Journal* in 1928, he wrote:

Ce journal que je me propose de tenir le plus régulièrement qu'il me sera possible, m'aidera, je crois, à voir plus clair en moi-même. C'est ma vie entière que je compte mettre en ces pages, avec une franchise et une exactitude absolues. [J, 1]

The Socratic quest, then, was instrumental in the birth of Green's diary. Fully aware of the duality of his nature, he wanted to commit himself to the discovery of his true identity. The desire to hide nothing and to be totally honest, perhaps an indication of Gide's tremendous influence during Green's separation from the Church, was too ambitious for the author to accomplish until he wrote the autobiography in the 1960s. His hesitation to speak frankly and candidly of his erotic difficulties prevented the sensual aspect of this radically sundered personality from asserting its true importance in the *Journal*. Appearing before a group of journalists in 1955, Green was asked why he hadn't revealed everything in his *Journal*. He replied that one should not confuse a journal with a public confession and that his was composed of selected passages taken from a more intimate journal.

Julien Green's *Journal* is first and foremost the spiritual record of his first self, the mystic that has persisted in his personality ever since the saintly aspirations of his childhood. The aspect of the *Journal* that comes next in importance is the picture of Green the artist that one gets from his reflections on his own writings and on the vocation of the novelist in general. Discussion of this motif I shall defer to Chapter Six, since it involves the conception of the third self, the visionary artist.

It has become a platitude among critics to say that Green has never felt the compulsion to become "engagé." Still, this statement remains one of the most significant ones that can be applied to him, and its significance is a convenient liaison between Green the mystic and Green the artist in the diary.

Je fuis avec horreur tout ce qui me rappelle que je suis au monde en ces temps détestables. . . . Ma place en 1940 n'est proprement nulle part sinon là où je puis me retirer du monde. [J, 364]

Chaque semaine me voit un peu plus désaccordé avec mon siècle. [J, 370]

Green the mystic has remained "désengagé" because he has lived in a spiritual reality that transcends worldly considerations. But Green the artist has refused to commit himself to a cause or a party for reasons of a different order.

He describes a conversation in which Gide tried to convince him that, sooner or later, he would be forced to choose from among the political factions of the time (J, 212-13). Green, of course, remained unshakable. An earlier entry in the *Journal* made it clear that his fiction would always remain apolitical:

Tout le monde se mêle de politique, sauf moi qui n'y entends rien. Je vis en me bouchant les oreilles, autrement je ne pourrais écrire. Je crois que le travail est une fin en soi et la publication d'un livre quelque chose de presque accidentel. [J, 88]

Green has refused to involve himself in political movements because he is engrossed in a realm that does not allow him the necessary leisure to *believe* in the "real" world.[4] He lives most profoundly in a visionary realm where he submits himself to the interminable conflict of the fictional reality, alternately besieged by the spirit and the flesh. The *Journal* contains countless statements of the author's incapacity to believe in the objective reality of the exterior world. "Ce monde n'est pas mon pays" (J, 162).

What is, indeed, Julien Green's country? He is an American citizen who has spent less than a decade of his life in the United States. Many of his French readers still do not realize he is a native Parisian. His fiction—whether its setting be Paris, the French provinces, the southern United States, or Copenhagen—takes place over and over again in an interior landscape where the clash of mystical aspirations and erotic obsessions constitutes the essential Greenian drama. It is the same drama of which Mallarmé was speaking when he defined the only true subject for the artist as "l'antagonisme de rêve chez l'homme avec les fatalités à son existence départies par le malheur."[5]

Perhaps the definitive statement on Green's country must come from his own works. In the play *L'Ennemi*, for example, Elisabeth tells Pierre that their country is not the earth; they are instead "les créatures du feu" (*L'Ennemi*, III, i). By the same token Green writes that "la nuit est un peu ma patrie" (J, 586). And Joseph Day says, "Je sais ce que c'est que le feu. Le feu est ma patrie" (*Moïra*, 208). Night is the realm that permits the mystic to see his visions, the realm of dreams that reveal mystical or obsessional worlds not accessible in daylight. Fire is the realm of desire, of conflict, the battlefield for the eternal antagonism of spiritual and erotic forces in Green's psyche.

The images of fire and of night are persistent motifs in Green's work, and they reveal one important strategy that motivates the two opposing Greenian selves, namely, escape. The erotic fantasies of the sensualist are a form of escape. In *L'Autre*, Roger explains his ungovernable sensuality as escape:

> Dans l'espèce de panique qui s'emparait de moi, je cherchais follement un refuge. Ni la boisson, ni les drogues n'avaient jamais eu d'empire sur mon cerveau. La peur, chez moi, ne s'abolissait que dans l'érotisme. [*L'Autre*, 77]

Denying the reality of the exterior world in favor of the mystical realm is another form of escape. Death is a truly obsessive theme, especially in the early works (e.g., *Les Clefs de la mort*, *Le Visionnaire*), and in describing the force of eroticism on his imagination, Green remarks that death is the most beautiful of all exotic lands.

The motive of escape is equally important in the sensual self and the mystical self. It explains Green's profoundly disengaged position among rival political and philosophical causes of our time, and it is a result of his inability to believe in the "real" world. At one point in the *Journal*, he compares the human condition to that of an insect crawling along a window pane in search of an opening that will permit it to fly off toward the firmament.

> Depuis quelques années, ce problème de la fenêtre qui ne veut pas s'ouvrir compte de plus en plus dans ma vie. D'une façon générale, c'est le problème de toute vie. S'échapper. [J, 294]

Here we are faced with a vitally important paradox in the psyche of Julien Green the artist. In the autobiography it is obvious that the exterior world had an irresistible attraction for the adolescent Green. In the *Journal*, however, we find Green's mystical self repulsed by the exterior world, and his fiction recounts his search for *la grande évasion* in various alternative worlds. The radical ambivalence of Green's attitude toward reality is one of the most revealing aspects of his basic duality. "Le monde est si beau qu'il faut un très grand effort pour s'en détacher, même quand on croit" (J, 705). A great novelist must, of necessity, be endowed with a sensitivity that is uniquely and profoundly affected by the exterior world. In order to appreciate the extent to which Green was captivated in his youth by the beauty of tangible reality, as opposed to the spiritual realm, we must turn to the book that offers the most complete picture of Green's childhood and youth, the autobiography.

Between *Chaque homme dans sa nuit* (1960) and *L'Autre* (1971), Julien Green published no novels. It was his longest absence from fiction since the beginning of his career. Aside from continuing his journal, he was occupied during that period mainly with a three-volume autobiography: *Partir avant le jour* (1963) begins with his earliest childhood remembrances and ends in 1917; *Mille chemins ouverts* (1964) recounts his World War I experiences in the American Field Service, the American Red Cross, and the French artillery; *Terre lointaine* (1966) covers his three years at the University of Virginia. After a hiatus of several years, Green returned to his autobiography and published a fourth volume, *Jeunesse*, in 1974.

The most striking aspect of the autobiography for one who is already familiar with Green's other confessional works (the *Journal* and *Memories of Happy Days*[6]) is the relative candor with which the author discusses the erotic aspect of his personality. In contrast to the reticence of the *Journal*, these volumes burn with the erotic intensity of eternal adolescence, in an almost Rimbaldian sense. Significantly, one of the few critical studies that appreciates the importance of the autobiography is subtitled *L'Obsession du mal* (by Jean Sémolué). Green wrote in the *Journal* on September 2, 1961, that he had placed at the beginning of his autobiography a personal reminder that read: "Tout dire ou se taire."

The basic conflict between spirit and flesh within Julien Green is the dilemma with which the autobiography deals. The tension created by this polarity is as strong here as in all of Green's works, and many of the references to it resemble those we find in the *Journal* or the fiction.

Je voulais tout à la fois le monde et le ciel. [MCO, 103]

Je voyais clairement le monde partagé entre le bien et le mal. . . . J'eus l'intuition subite qu'une longue guerre s'engageait entre moi-même et moi-même. [TL, 111-12]

It is the emphasis on the erotic aspect in Green's duality that makes the autobiography a unique part of his literary production. Even his spiritual aspirations are examined from the perspective of the carnal realm. Looking back on his adolescence, he realizes that even his faith was, to a great extent, of a sensual nature. "Mon âme elle-même avait cinq sens" (TL, 191). The spiritual and sensual are inextricably interwoven in Green's personality. He says in the *Journal* that we are susceptible to the most dangerous temptations at the moment of the most exalting transports of the soul.

Partir avant le jour is a veritable wealth of material for the psychoanalyst.[7] It is an intense evocation of the mysterious origins of Green's inner turmoil. He abjures the strictly chronological approach of traditional autobiography and proceeds by means of a method very similar to that of the psychoanalyst's free-association. For this reason, his autobiography is most profoundly the record of the development of the forces that for a long time lay dormant in his subconscious.

Si je n'y mettais sans cesse bon ordre, ce livre tomberait dans l'autobiographie pure et simple. Or, c'est bien autre chose que je désire. Je me propose de regarder là où je n'ai jamais tourné les yeux que par hasard, je veux tâcher de voir clair dans cette partie de la conscience qui demeure si souvent obscure à mesure que nous nous éloignons de notre enfance. [PAJ, 96-97]

In one sense, *Partir avant le jour* leads us to interpret the autobiography as an indictment of the puritanical method of education that has led to so much anxiety in Green. Actually young Julien received far less Protestant training than his older sisters, who memorized the Anglican catechism and were confirmed in the Anglican Church in Paris. Green himself claims that "le protestantisme m'effleura à peine" (PAJ, 66).

The importance of Protestantism in Green's development, then, can best be described as relative. Protestantism was only one facet of the significance of the mother in Green's personality. The principal source of Green's anxiety was not the thorn of puritanism, but rather the ambivalent influence of his mother, whose presence is felt either consciously or unconsciously throughout *Partir avant le jour*, even after her death in 1914.

Mary Hartridge Green was a well-loved and loving person. Her spiritual sensitivity and compassion, doubtless, were among the gifts that she passed on to her son, but her influence on young Julien also had undesirable effects. From *Partir avant le jour* it is evident that in all her desire to make life happy for her son, she nevertheless was responsible for much of the turmoil that later reached neurotic proportions. On one hand, she represented security, love, and warmth.

Quand j'étais seul avec quelqu'un qui me parlait doucement dans une langue que je ne comprenais pas, je savais que c'était la personne qui m'aimait plus que les autres. [PAJ, 24]

Very soon she became the person who represented religion in the life of the young boy. She read the Bible to the children every evening (in the King James Version that still holds its powerful effect on Green), she sent them to the Anglican Church, and she recited with little Julien the Lord's Prayer in English. Her native tongue became for her youngest child the language in which one communicated with the Lord. He incessantly questioned his mother, "cette mère qui me parlait pour Dieu" (PAJ, 67). She heard him crying in bed one night, and when she came to him he asked her whether he was saved. "Tu as la foi. Tu es sauvé" (PAJ, 29), she assured him, and he went off to sleep.[8]

Despite the love and security provided by Mrs. Green, the young Julien's feelings for her and her effect on him began to show signs of dangerous aberrations. It was acknowledged that she loved him more than the other children, he being the youngest. She watched over him not only with tenderness but also with suspicious solicitude. He began to see his mother not as a person but as a god.

Dans l'espèce de crépuscule où je me trouvais encore, cette présence de ma mère prenait peu à peu un caractère magique, et à la distance de toute une vie, le souvenir de sa voix me fait encore battre le coeur. [PAJ, 24]

The child began to depend too heavily on his mother—"Je ne me plaisais vraiment qu'avec elle" (PAJ, 25). He pursued her with incessant protestations of "I love you." Inevitably, this tendency resulted in a fully developed oedipal complex, which is quite obvious in an imaginary adventure serial that the young Green resumed for himself in bed each night. He would imagine himself the youngest of an enormous family that was scattered all over the globe. In order to exterminate the entire family, he would undertake long and difficult journeys. His mother was the only one to find grace in his murderous designs. He adds that in time, these fantasies were transposed into his fiction.[9]

Mrs. Green's fear and hatred for the sexual instinct were gradually transferred to her son in various ways, sometimes in the most classically oedipal situations. At an age of no more than four or five years, he was discovered in bed with his hands in the forbidden position. His mother ran to the kitchen and returned with the bread knife crying, "I'll cut it off!" His mother was already keeping a close watch over him because of the horror that she felt for manifestations of sexuality, which she regarded as sinful.

It was his mother who gave him his evening bath. In giving him explicit directions as to how to perform the operation, she inevitably encountered the fearful term "le corps," and looking at her son's unclothed body with an expression of repulsion, she could not refrain from commenting, "Oh, que c'est donc laid!" (PAJ, 84-85). Such episodes had a permanent effect on the psychological background of Green's future works.

> Quelque chose en moi était atteint d'une manière incompréhensible. Je pouvais avoir onze ans et mon innocence était profonde. Ma mère me regarda tristement comme on regarde un coupable, qu'on ne peut pas punir parce qu'on l'aime trop, et quand je me fus rhabillé, elle me serra dans ses bras. [PAJ, 85-86]

Near the end of her life, Mrs. Green revealed to her son one of the keys to her fear of sexuality. She told him of her beloved brother Willie whom she had left in Savannah when the Greens moved from Georgia. The last time she had seen him, he was mentally and physically ravaged by a venereal disease. The sight of her once-beautiful brother, then only a ghost of his former self, had been a shattering experience for Mary Green and a revelation of God's wrathful vengeance upon the transgressors of the flesh. The memory of Uncle Willie's fate became for Julien the dreadful risk that one incurred in sexual relationships and was a contributing factor in rendering him incapable of normal sexual development.

> Alors, maintenant, tout est beaucoup plus clair. Je comprends mieux cette mère épouvantée par un souvenir ineffaçable, veillant sur son garçon, guettant avec horreur les premières indications de sensualité, d'une sensualité que Dieu avait maudite dans la personne de son frère. Je comprends, sans sourire, le couteau à pain. [PAJ, 211]

Although the conflict of spirit and flesh is portrayed primarily from the perspective of the carnal realm in the autobiography, there are frequent indications of the continuous power of spirituality in Green's early youth. The erotic side of his personality was still largely dormant, and for the most part Green remembers his childhood as a very happy one. As a boy, he sometimes found himself invaded by a brief experience of mystical happiness.

One of Green's first memories is one of "une minute de ravissement" that has never been surpassed. While playing alone on the floor of his parents' dimly lit room, he looked through the window at the dark sky and the shining stars.

J'eus ce que je ne puis appeler qu'un élan d'amour. J'ai aimé en ce monde, mais jamais comme en ce court moment, et je ne savais qui j'aimais. Pourtant, je savais qu'il était là et que me voyant il m'aimait aussi. [PAJ, 16]

Some time later Green found himself alone in an enclosed garden on a cool autumn morning. As he stood motionless for a moment with the cool air on his face, he heard someone beating out a rug nearby and a piano playing a Mozart selection that he had heard his sister Mary play. As he listened to these sounds, a thought came into his mind that he was unable to formulate. It was a strange feeling to be standing in the garden with the coolness on his face and the secret, ineffable "bonheur de vivre" in his heart.

In June of his eighth year, Julien was seated in his classroom at Janson-de-Sailly. Gazing out the window at the metal roof of an adjacent building, he experienced another sudden inexplicable moment of happiness.

Je fus tout à coup arraché à moi-même. Pendant plusieurs minutes, j'eus la certitude qu'il existait un autre monde que celui que je voyais autour de moi, et que cet autre monde était vrai. [PAJ, 80]

With no intentions of impugning the spiritual authenticity of these experiences, one may consider them as manifestations of the motive of escape in Green's works. Each of these three *moments privilégiés* incorporates a typical pattern of escape. The child in each case finds himself in an enclosed area, and the stimulus that induces his spiritual rapture comes from outside the enclosure. The ambivalent image of claustration may take various forms: a garden, a room, a house, and it inevitably recalls the archetype of the womb in an oedipal situation such as Green's. There is security in Uncle Will Mackall's ancestral home in Virginia: "un petit univers clos de toute part et protégé des menaces de l'extérieur" (TL, 43). But the enclosed rectangular arrangement of the buildings and galleries of the University of Virginia gives the impression of "un monde inconnu, fermé et protégé de toutes parts, inquiétant malgré tout" (TL, 19).

The painful solitude that resulted from maternal dominance is referred to as a "cercle magique" (TL, 24) that Green was unable to escape. The houses in *Mont-Cinère* and *Adrienne Mesurat* have the importance of a principal character[10] in creating a stifling atmosphere of claustration from which escape is possible only through death or madness. In discussing his earliest writings as a university student, Green gives evidence of the importance of the motif of escape. In his first narratives, he often depicted himself pursued on a staircase and taking refuge in a basement, a motif that was also prevalent in his dreams.

At the same time that Julien was being initiated into a mystical realm, he was also being invaded by a different but equally mysterious presence. Near the age of five, there was what he calls "une catastrophe dont le sens m'échappe" (PAJ, 22), namely, the sudden consciousness of his individual existence.

Tous les hommes ont connu cet instant singulier où l'on se sent brusquement séparé du reste du monde par le fait qu'on est soi-même et non ce qui nous entoure. . . . Certes je fus heureux par la suite, mais non comme je l'étais auparavant, dans l'Eden d'où nous sommes chassés par l'ange fulgurant qui s'appelle Moi. [PAJ, 23]

Along with this conceptual loss of innocence one finds in Green's early years a tendency to feel the presence of evil in a disturbingly concrete way. There is frequent mention of the belief in ghosts and spirits among his sisters, and he describes a terrifying "game" that he often played in front of his parents' closet. This was the special sanctuary where the devil kept himself. The child would come to the closet, call the demon three times, and flee in terror at the moment when he thought he saw the garments move and part themselves in order to permit Satan to reveal himself.

On his walks with his sisters there was a hideous blind beggar whom little Julien always saw as they crossed the Pont de Saint-Cloud. Subsequently, whenever he went to what he called "le petit endroit," he could not help imagining that the frightening beggar was behind him (PAJ, 27-28).

The young Green was taken to the popular Guignol de la Muette puppet shows. But his reaction was one of horror at the end of the show when a marionette dressed in black made his appearance armed with "une batte homicide" with which he proceeded to punish the other characters. "Je croyais voir s'ouvrir la porte de la penderie et le diable apparaître sous les traits de ce tout petit personnage qui devenait soudain immense" (PAJ, 31).

By far the most seductive revelation of evil for Green, both as a child and as a young man, was the power that the visual image exerted on his sensibility. This is a motif that extends from *Partir avant le jour* through the entire autobiography. The representation of the beauty of the body (usually male), or of the face in painting and sculpture always had a violent effect on Green's psychological equilibrium. He writes that he was hardly old enough to speak when "the enemy" began to cast his shadow on him in this way. The six-year-old Green examined with fear and admiration the splendid suffering bodies with which Gustave Doré had peopled Dante's *Inferno*. Stunned by the violent display of nudity, the child feverishly traced in his own turn the shapes of those perfect forms, which were to determine forever his erotic nature.

Pendant de longues minutes, je m'enivrai de la vision magique que je voulais saisir et posséder en la cernant de ce gros trait noir, vaine et violente caresse dont j'ai gardé toute ma vie la brûlure. [PAJ, 47]

The one painting that affected Green as a child more seriously than any other visual image was Lecomte du Nouy's "Les Porteurs de mauvaises nouvelles."[11] It depicts a pharoah lounging on his couch and staring into the distance, oblivious to the flimsily clad corpses of three black slaves whom he has just executed because of the unfavorable news they have brought. Green's reaction was graphically hallucinatory:

J'imaginai qu'un de ces grands corps bruns foudroyés par la mort gisait véritablement sous mes yeux, et il me semble que tout mon être, âme et chair, se jetait sur lui. [PAJ, 49-50]

Visits to the Louvre caused in Green a kind of sexual intoxication that he could not understand. No one explained why nudity, which was damned as a terrible sin, was being glorified and set upon pedestals for all to admire. He later suffered the same torture when his sister Mary sent him a postcard from Rome with a picture of one of Michelangelo's *ignudi* of the Sistine Chapel. Jean Sémolué sees in Green's description of the figure a model for an obsessive character-type in Green's writings.[12] Indeed, the proud beauty of the body crowned by tousled locks of hair characterizes both the statues and Claude in *L'Autre sommeil*, Serge in *Minuit*, and Ghéza in *Chaque homme dans sa nuit*. Julien was so taken with the picture on the postcard that he copied it very carefully in his drawing album.

On his first trip to the United States by way of Italy, he was impressed by the beauty of a bronze Narcissus in the museum at Naples. He ordered a miniature of it, and as he later contemplated it in his room in Savannah, he was ashamed of "l'impur" but also felt "une joie furieuse" (TL, 110). The same feeling is described earlier in seeing the statues of the Greek gods in the Louvre:

Impassibles ces dieux, mais comme on souffrait devant eux et dans cette souffrance, quel bizarre plaisir. On souffrait et on ne voulait pas s'arrêter de souffrir. [MCO, 244]

One other revealing indication of the significance of the visual image for Green was evident in his favorite childhood and adolescent pastime of drawing. From his descriptions of the drawings, it is clear that they were expressions of the sexual fantasies at work within him. All the major themes of his fiction were present in a raw and primitive manner. Taking his cue from Doré, for example, he drew a group of naked men and women being pursued by a torturer who was lashing them with a whip. The idea occurred to him that these people were being punished for their nudity. His emotional state during the time he was drawing is startling:

Il me semble que je me jetais tout entier dans mon dessin, et par l'effet d'une sorte d'hallucination, je devenais ce que je dessinais, je le devenais avec une joie sauvage qui m'en faisait mordre ma langue. [PAJ, 51]

Later he describes again the strange exaltation that took hold of him while he was drawing and his identification with the characters in the pictures. Elaborating on the invasion of demonic forces within him while making the drawings, he discovers a reality in itself, a whole new world of frightening proportions. When he drew nude figures instead of such mundane subjects as a parade, for example, he felt himself passing from the ordinary world into a secret world, one that he harbored inside himself and that he wanted to see on paper. At those moments, he would feel a mysterious presence. "Il y avait quelqu'un avec moi, cela, j'en suis sûr" (PAJ, 91).

These were the first indications in the young Green of the transformations of the self that were to become so important to his later career as novelist. Even as a child, the act of expressing in concrete form the erotic and spiritual fantasies that were seething within him gave him such a feeling of exaltation that he was beginning to discover a third self, a *moi profond*. With this in mind we have little trouble understanding the phenomenon of the adult Green's purging himself of his obsessions by transposing them into fiction. In fact, there are intermediate stages of development in the process, such as the scene in *Mille chemins ouverts* where he recalls having compulsively written several pages "d'une obscénité maladive":

> Le sang courait sous la peau, la chair vivait. En une seconde, je rejoignis les hallucinations de ma sixième année et le mal se glissait dans mon cerveau comme dans les couloirs d'un palais dont il retrouve le chemin. [MCO, 96]

Drawing, then, for the young Green was "le rêve du corps" (PAJ, 94). As evidence of the continued need to convert his inner turmoil into visual form it might be observed at this point that Green's first effort to engage himself in a nonreligious vocation was an aborted attempt at painting. The visual image in all its manifestations represents the attraction of the sensuous realm as opposed to the mystic's invisible reality. It is with reason that Green has applied Gautier's famous remark to himself: "Je suis un homme pour qui le monde extérieur existe" (J, 434).

What are the elements of the various forms of the visual image that evoke in Green such a hallucinatory reaction? First, there is the connection of nudity with guilt and punishment, as in Doré's illustrations, in "Les Porteurs de mauvaises nouvelles," and in the childhood drawings. "Le crime, c'était de ne pas avoir de vêtements, le crime, c'était d'aller nu. Ainsi les hommes que je dessinais étaient des criminels" (PAJ, 94). Mrs. Green's disgust for her son's nudity in the bath scene is intimately related to this progression of ideas. As a result of her horror, the young Julien naturally was at once more intensely fascinated and repulsed by nudity. During his wartime service he was haunted by the presence of a mirror in his room and finally succumbed to the temptation to look at his own naked body. As he removed his clothing, he was certain that he was committing a sin. When he saw his reflection, he rushed up to the cold image and kissed its lips (MCO, 76-79).

From the equivalence of nudity with damnation it is not difficult to infer the connection of eroticism with suffering. Indeed, the suffering in the visual images that acted on Green and the suffering (mixed with pleasure) that they induced within him are involved in a complex erotic strategy of sadism, masochism, and oedipal anxiety. Sadomasochism is an important motif in all Green's works. It is evident in many of the passages I have discussed, such as the Guignol de la Muette shows and the childhood drawings.[13] The hallucination in which Julien exterminates all of his relatives except his mother (PAJ, 206) should also be recalled at this point, and it is interesting to observe that he reports having written a sonnet on Saint Julien-le-Pauvre (PAJ, 312-13). In Flaubert's legend of Saint Julien, Green's patron saint was plagued with a similar case of *dédoublement* and escaped his own "cercle magique" by means of hunts in which the killing reached hallucinatory proportions. In order to expiate the sin of parricide, he spent the last half of his life in a long period of ascetic suffering.

Desire and hatred are very difficult to distinguish in the violent temperament of Julien Green, as we shall see more clearly in the discussion of his fiction in later chapters.

Un meurtrier dort au fond de nous-mêmes. . . . Je dévorais mes colères. La fureur qui si souvent bouillonnait en moi rejoignait sans doute une faim sexuelle qui ne devait se manifester que beaucoup plus tard. [MCO, 28]

In this connection, he notes the ambivalence of his emotions during a fight with an Army friend whose beauty he had admired during occupational duty in Germany (MCO, 212-13). And later, in analyzing his feelings for young men at the university who had aroused his desire, he asked himself what he would have done with them.

Je me répondais à moi-même que je serais leur esclave ou qu'ils seraient les miens. Le mot d'esclave revenait sans cesse dans mon esprit à leur propos, parce que je le trouvais beau et qu'il évoquait des plaisirs inconnus où la douleur se mêlait à la férocité. [TL, 162]

Throughout the autobiographical narrative, it is obvious that Green's youth was fraught with anxiety. Moreover, it was a disturbingly mysterious anxiety, since it stemmed from two different problems that are easily confused. The spiritual uneasiness evident in the child's waking at night to ask tearfully for his mother to reassure him of his salvation may be partially motivated by abnormal need of the mother's attention and affection. During the war he did not flinch at physical danger. "Ma peur était d'une autre sorte. Je tremblais devant Dieu, de là cette espèce de panique devant le péché" (MCO, 27). At the university, on the other hand, he dreamed one night that there was a serpent in his bed. The appearance of reality in the dream was so complete that it took him a quarter-hour of reasoning with himself in the light before he could go back to bed. "Fallait-il voir dans cette bête à la fois si terrifiante et si belle une représentation du mal? Le fait est que je tremblais devant le mal" (TL, 269-70).

Long before Mrs. Green told her son the frightening story of her brother Willie, her anxieties were transmitted in more subtle ways. From her he learned that the body was the enemy but also the temple of the Holy Spirit. The flesh thus took on added significance: "L'intégrité du corps se liait à l'intégrité de l'âme. Il fallait demeurer intact" (PAJ, 86-87). While bathing her son one day, Mrs. Green gave a start and exclaimed, "Ces taches rouges! Qu'est-ce que c'est?" Answering her own question, she sobbed, "La lèpre!" and had the whole family in an uproar until the doctor came to allay her fears. It is little wonder that the only thing Green remembers about one of his first *lyçée* teachers is a phrase alluding to the horrors of sickness. The spectre of Uncle Willie was one of the images that flashed through the adolescent Green's mind when his brother-in-law made subtle attempts to encourage heterosexual involvement.

The young Green's fear of the ocean—"La mer . . . me fit immédiatement horreur" (PAJ, 151)—was perhaps a form of anxiety in reaction to a hostile maternal symbol. His fear of swimming was closely related to the prohibitions on nudity that had been imposed on his mind. His attempts to repress the "cauchemar de la sexualité" (TL, 67) demonstrate just how serious his erotic anxieties were. "Il y avait ceci de particulier dans mes représentations de personnages nus, c'est qu'aucun d'eux n'avait de sexe"

(PAJ, 96). A reproduction in one of his parents' art books depicted a beautiful Roman slave, completely naked, who was busy with her toilette. But what especially impressed Green was the fact that her body had no trace of sex.

J'avais sous les yeux l'image d'un être idéal, beau, mince, svelte et totalement asexué. Or, cet être, je le voulais et je le voulais tellement que pris d'inquiétude comme si je commettais un péché, je tournais la page. J'aurais voulu que l'humanité entière, hommes et femmes, fût comme la petite esclave. [MCO, 262-63]

The result of Mary Hartridge Green's influence on her son was a spiritual and erotic dilemma that kept his psyche in continual chaos. She was the definitive object of his love because of her overprotectiveness. He inherited from her a spiritual fervor that denied the importance of the real world and a rigid moral standard that was characterized by a deep fear and hatred for the sexual instinct. These influences inhibited normal sexual development in the adolescent Green, and after his mother's death he found himself entrenched in a near-impenetrable solitude.

Je me croyais, non supérieur à autrui, mais différent. Je ne faisais partie, à mes propres yeux, d'aucun groupe. Au-dessus de moi, pareille à un ange attentif, il y avait ma mère qui prenait la place de la vie. [PAJ, 261]

One of the principal explanations for Green's solitude was his prolonged innocence and amazing ignorance of sexual life. "Sans doute, mon ignorance bâtissait autour de moi une prison solide" (TL, 127). There were traumatic encounters with sexuality that began during his *lyçée* years at Janson-de-Sailly. When he was twelve he witnessed a scene of precocious exhibitionism that one boy performed in front of the class while the teacher was out of the room.

Plus étonnant que tout me paraît aujourd'hui la facilité avec laquelle cette scène s'effaça de mon esprit. Elle m'avait fait peur, mais je l'oubliai et je l'oubliai pendant des années. [PAJ, 100]

Two years later there was an episode in which three classmates seduced him in a train compartment. Again, the terrifying scene that should have been a revelation to the young boy was erased from his memory for years. Throughout numerous other traumas in his youth, Green demonstrated a persistent facility of systematic repression that preserved a kind of sexual innocence in him.

The solitude of the adolescent Green was again the result of his mother's influence in the concept of purity that she instilled in him. He made a law for himself that no one was to touch him.

A mes yeux, le corps était quelque chose de saint et ne souffrait aucun attouchement. . . . J'étais pur. . . . Il y avait autour de moi une sorte de zone interdite que je m'étais créée et dont la réalité finissait par se faire sentir. [PAJ, 132]

To refuse to allow himself to be touched was one means of avoiding sexual involvement. The same strategy was evident after his decision to become a religious when he began to inform everyone of his vocation. He chose to keep himself apart, alone, pure. His solitude began to take on the proportions of the pathological solipsism that is characteristic of many of his fictional protagonists. Speaking of his prolonged innocence, he states that

un curé de campagne m'eût expliqué en deux minutes que j'étais la proie de rêveries, mais il n'y avait personne pour me parler. . . . J'étais seul. . . . Comme le poète, j'étais hanté, et je l'étais d'autant plus gravement que cette ardeur inapaisée demeurait surtout cérébrale. [MCO, 242-43]

The inevitable consequences of prolonged sexual innocence, mystical reveries, and solipsism in the young Green were devastating when he was exposed to military life and the university experience. No longer accorded the excessive protection of being the *benjamin* of a large, affectionate family, he received the shock of the real world with its full impact. The middle two volumes of the autobiography trace the slow maturation of the latent homosexual desires in the author. There is a long series of young men whose beauty was a source of torture for Green.

During his service as an ambulance driver for the American Field Service, for example, he suffered from his attraction for a new driver named Jack who joined the section in Italy. He was struck especially with Jack's blond hair, the "visage d'ange rose aux lèvres charnues," and "l'extraordinaire beauté de son corps qu'on devinait sous ses vêtements" (MCO, 98). Jack's only unattractive attribute was his obscene language. Understandably, Green avoided Jack because he was both "charmant et odieux"

(MCO, 99). One morning the young Green found Jack asleep and took advantage of the opportunity to admire his beauty.

Je demeurai immobile sur le seuil et le coeur me bâttit à grands coups. N'était-ce pas un désir étrange que celui de me pencher sur le dormeur et de poser ma joue sur sa joue que le sommeil rendait encore plus rose qu'à l'ordinaire? . . . Il me parut si beau que j'en éprouvai une joie mêlée de frayeur, mais je ne pouvais m'expliquer ni la joie, ni la frayeur. [MCO, 100]

Green insists that at that point in his life such experiences were chaste. Much of the erotic turbulence within him was still dormant. Sexual frenzy was alien and disgusting, but the beauty of a face could devastate him.

The facility for systematic repression of sexual experiences explains Green's conviction that such experiences were chaste. The angelism to which he aspired resulted in a system of masochistic repression designed to enable him to remain pure without turning away totally from his nascent homosexuality. In a subconscious way, he found pleasure in repression.

During the occupation of Germany as an *aspirant* in the French artillery, Green shared a room with another attractive young man. One night he was taken with the desire to join his companion in the bed, but managed to resist. Later a quarrel led to a fight that Green described with erotic overtones, adding that the episode was to become an important source of both *Moïra* and *Sud*.

Green's long-repressed homosexual nature did not assert itself without a ravaging struggle. His deep spirituality would not permit him to plunge with abandon into the delirium of sensualism, but his physical and intellectual maturation at the University of Virginia amounted, in effect, to an undeniable discovery of his erotic self. He describes an episode during his first year at Virginia in which his desires were still quite chaste. The sight of the young man who was driving him in his wagon to his uncle's house[14] evoked in Green a painfully ambivalent reaction:

Je regarde mon voisin et j'ai l'impression que mes entrailles se serrent. Pourquoi souffre-t-on rien qu'à voir un visage humain? On peut regarder et regarder, souffrir et encore souffrir, mais dans cette souffrance il y a un bonheur cruel qui ravage le coeur. [TL, 38-39]

In Dr. Fitzhugh's Latin class at the university, the subject of pederasty inevitably arose during discussion of Virgil. The professor expressed a regrettably dogmatic attitude on the subject, referring to it as "la honte de l'antiquité" (TL, 53). Green's surprising naïveté is evident in the thoughts that occurred to him at that moment.

> Je compris que la passion étrange dont parlait Virgile habitait aussi en moi. Un trait de lumière éclaira toute ma vie. J'eus peur de cette révélation qui me montrait pareil aux jeunes gens de l'antiquité. Dans le monde moderne, j'étais seul à éprouver cet amour inquiétant. . . . Ce jour-là je refermai mon livre avec un sentiment d'horreur à laquelle se mêlait je ne sais quoi de plus profond et de plus sourd, une vague et cruelle satisfaction. [TL, 54]

The objects of Green's fearful desires during his college years began to divide themselves into two quite distinct types: young men whose beautiful faces inspired in him a kind of Platonic desire that carried with it no feeling of shame, and those who caused him to burn with a passion that entailed terrifying prohibitions, guilt, and remorse. In his mind, love could only be pure. Desire was a different thing altogether. It was, quite simply, sinful.

The passion that is most fully recounted in *Terre lointaine* is Julien's long-tacit admiration of a certain Mark S., whom he succeeded in approaching only near the end of his stay at the university. This relationship is typical of those that come under the category of Platonic love.

> Je n'éprouvais aucun désir pour Mark, simplement une monstrueuse tendresse. Je rêvais que, m'agenouillant devant lui, je prenais ses deux mains pour les mettre sur mon visage, je rêvais que, me relevant, il me serrait dans ses bras et me permettait de lui dire que je l'aimais. [TL, 103]

Green makes an explicit contrast between his feelings for Mark and his reaction to the nude statue of Hermes that stood just outside one of his classrooms. The force that took hold of him upon seeing the Hermes was desire, an emotion that belonged only in the realm of the impure. It was of an altogether different essence from his love for Mark, which he never felt the need to mention in confession. To Julien, Saint Paul's condemnation of homosexuality in Romans 1: 27 could not apply to his relationship with Mark. "Mon amour était . . . un amour où je ne voyais pas de tache" (TL, 113). Reinforcing the distinction between love and desire—one that takes on immense significance in much of his fiction—Green contrasts his feelings for Mark with those he had for a young man he encountered at the family residence in Virginia. A splendid physical specimen usually dressed in his sailor's uniform, Ted exerted on Julien a terrifying force of corruption. "Je n'aimais pas Ted comme j'aimai Mark. Ted, c'était le mal sous son aspect le plus séduisant" (TL, 120).

By the end of *Terre lointaine*, it is clear that the mystical aspect of Green's duality was suffering at the expense of his sensual nature. The invasion of the realm of the flesh brought about "le grand refus" (J, 385) of a religious vocation. The period of Green's life that ensued (1922-1928) was the period of erotic involvement and religious alienation. These years are recounted—although with notably less dramatic intensity than in the first three volumes—in *Jeunesse*, the sequel added by Green in 1974. However, it was also an essential stage in his spiritual development, not to mention his development as a novelist. In describing the inhibiting force of his adolescent innocence, Green states that "le péché brisa ce cercle magique beaucoup plus tard. Ce fut par le péché que je retrouvai l'humanité" (PAJ, 132).

The angelism of Green's adolescent spiritual aspirations was never to be outgrown. The rest of his life Green was obliged to live with a bitter nostalgia for lost sainthood. But he was on the verge of discovering a vocation that would afford him a means of coming to grips with his most disturbing problems, both the spiritual anxiety of the mystic and the sexual obsessions of the sensualist.

Chapter Two

The Pilgrim's Descent: *Le Voyageur sur la terre*

In the fictional context of Julien Green's works, we find again the two rival aspects of the Greenian personality which dominated in the autobiographical context, the mystic and the sensualist. The duality of mystical and erotic themes characterizes the fiction to just as great an extent as the nonfiction. It is in this context, however, that Green begins to discover a third self and to open up an entirely new reality for which his career as a writer has destined him. The myth of the *moi profond* is incarnated in his fiction in such a way as to transcend the vicious circle of mystical and erotic forces. It is here that we may witness the most dramatic metamorphoses of the self in Julien Green.

In analyzing Green's fiction, I shall proceed chronologically, choosing a few specific works on which to concentrate and alluding from time to time to most of the others. For each representative novel or play, I shall discuss the three selves of Julien Green, assessing in turn the relative importance of mystical and erotic elements and attempting to elucidate the development of the *moi profond*.

Naturally, my discussion of the mystical aspect of Green's fiction will incorporate traditional mystical doctrine, while the erotic dimension will call for psychoanalytical theory. These two disciplines share important analogous principles[1] to such an extent that their combination is well suited to the critic's task of interpreting Julien Green's work. The author himself draws incisive analogies between the behavior of the saint and that of the sensualist. Paraphrasing Saint John of the Cross he observes that

> la nature humaine aspirant à Dieu, il est inévitable que dans cette exaltation vers le bien il n'y ait aussi et simultanément une sorte de marée montante de désirs charnels. . . . Cela explique que les tentations puissent être si fortes au moment des plus grands élans vers Dieu. [J, 375]

And as we shall see, most of his principal fictional characters (Elisabeth in *Minuit*, Wilfred in *Chaque homme dans sa nuit*, Karin in *L'Autre*, for example) are haunted by a mysterious force that expresses itself at times as the attraction of a transcendent realm and at other times as the persistent weight of erotic obsessions. The extent to which Green resolves this conflict by realizing the myth of the *moi profond* demonstrates how essential the transformations of the self in the fictional reality are to the stability of the Greenian personality.

As I went on, I got farther and farther away from my own actual experience as a student at the University of Virginia and watched with interest the picture becoming darker and weirder; it was like losing one's way in a wood and realizing by slow degrees that the wood is haunted. [*Memories of Happy Days*, 264-65]

These are the terms Green used to describe what was on his mind during the writing of his first fictional narrative in French, *Le Voyageur sur la terre* (1926).[2] The notion of disorientation in a sinister realm aptly describes the atmosphere of most of his early novels. In *Minuit* (1936) and *Le Visionnaire* (1934), for example, the supernatural element plays a predominant part in the story. It is an ambivalent kind of supernatural: on the one hand sinister and threatening to the protagonist's sanity and security, and evocative on the other hand of an unknowable deliverance.

The obsessions that people the psyche of the main character in the narratives of this period are only vaguely identified. They are just beginning to emerge from Green's subconscious and to be exorcised in the therapeutic activity of writing. The preoccupations of a spiritual nature are glossed over during this period of alienation from religion, and the sexual problems of the writer are too traumatic to explore voluntarily and consciously. The novels and stories of Green's first stage are largely a means of escape from the unresolved tension of spirituality and eroticism. Significantly, he states that in writing *Mont-Cinère*, for example, he tried to make the characters as much unlike himself as possible. That is one explanation for the abundance of female protagonists in Green's early works (*Adrienne Mesurat*, *Minuit*, *Le Visionnaire*). The literary style to which he first aspired was one in which there would be as few peculiarities as possible to call attention to the personality of the writer: an unobtrusive style that would hide the identity of the author.

The aim of the young novelist's "invisible" style was inevitably unreachable. The problems that were most profoundly affecting him found their way into his fiction in one form or another. Most of the main characters in this first period are led to some grave crime. Adrienne Mesurat pushes her father down the staircase to his death. Jean in *Les Clefs de la mort* tries repeatedly to summon enough courage to stab Clément Jalon. Emily Fletcher first tries to strangle her daughter and finally kills both herself and her daughter in the fire that destroys Mont-Cinère. Paul Guéret brutally beats the girl who refuses to give herself to him in *Léviathan*.

Green has often said that the natural result of unchecked eroticism is crime (e.g., *Journal*, Oct. 27, 1958; Oct. 18, 1966). Free-floating guilt and anxiety haunt the protagonists of Green's first novels long before they commit crimes. The crimes they either commit or meditate are emblematic of the guilt that Green felt for the eroticist's life he was leading at the time both as fantasy and in reality. The full-length novels of Green's first stage were examples of what André Rousseaux calls *réalisme magique*. The decor of the novels and the incidents that occur are not so much out of the ordinary. They conform to a relatively mimetic standard of reality. But they are always informed with a distinct atmosphere of the supernatural. The weird aura of *réalisme magique* that led many to compare Green to Hawthorne and the Brontës in this stage, and the intentionally unautobiographical criminal-protagonists were the fictional form that Green's escape adopted.

In *Le Voyageur sur la terre*, the spiritual preoccupations of the writer are mirrored in Daniel O'Donovan, but the erotic conflict is obscured. In *L'Autre sommeil*, the erotic problem takes precedence while spirituality is less evident. These two *nouvelles* retain the atmosphere of magic realism but are more overtly concerned with the struggle between spirituality and sexuality in the author than the other novels of the period.

The title of Green's *nouvelle, Le Voyageur sur la terre*, is taken from the eleventh chapter of Hebrews, where Saint Paul cites the great Old Testament figures as examples of faith.

These all died in faith, not having received the promises, but having seen them afar off, and were persuaded of them, and embraced them, and confessed that they were strangers and pilgrims on the earth. . . . But now they desire a better country, that is, an heavenly. [Heb. 11:13-16, KJV]

The pilgrim on the earth, searching in faith for the ultimate dwelling-place of the soul, is the mystic Daniel O'Donovan, whose spiritual quest will be seen to take on mythological proportions. The story of Daniel O'Donovan reveals the mythology of Green's personal spiritual quest in the same way that the *Divine Comedy* describes Dante's quest in mythological trappings. The pilgrimages of the *Comedy* and of *Le Voyageur* may be interpreted both as individual spiritual development and as metaphorical representations of the universal experience of spiritual development.

The story is set in an unnamed American town whose description very easily identifies it as Savannah, the home of Green's benefactor uncle, Walter Hartridge. Fairfax, the university town where Daniel O'Donovan travels to pursue his studies, is clearly patterned after Charlottesville.

Daniel is a young man who finds himself in the situation of adolescent claustration. An orphan, he lives in the house of his uncle, Thomas Drayton, a sour recluse who combines Voltairian deism with Rousseauistic ideas on education in the lectures he pompously delivers to his nephew. Mrs. Drayton is an incessant carper who never tires of complaining about the shortcomings of her husband and the difficulty of keeping the Christian virtue of patience with such a man. The last member of the household is Mrs. Drayton's father, a crotchety old fellow who likes to remind everyone that he served under General Jackson in the War Between the States. *Le capitaine* is revered by his daughter and bitterly resented by Mr. Drayton. The domestic testiness of the Draytons is similar to the hostility that reigns in the avarice-ridden family of *Mont-Cinère*, the tyranny of le père Mesurat, and the mutual distrust of Philippe, Henriette, and Éliane in *Epaves*.

Daniel has been received by this family quite unwillingly, and none of the people with whom he lives inspire any confidence in him. In his aunt's neurotic ramblings, he senses something that makes him strangely uneasy around her. As for his uncle, "Dans son visage décharné et vieilli je ne découvre rien d'un esprit généreux, rien d'un coeur charitable; tout y trahit la défiance, l'ennui et l'amertume d'un solitaire qui hait sa solitude" (Voy, 15).

Le capitaine's nightly mounting of the stairway[3] conjures up terrifying spectres in Daniel's imagination. Daniel's room, "la chambre la plus incommode" (Voy, 8), is located next to an abandoned one that he believes to be haunted. The view from his window is obscured by the depressing sight of the neighboring Presbyterian Church, which once was partly destroyed by a fire in which the steeple fell and burned down the house that had originally stood on the site of the Draytons' house. The new steeple of the church is a source of anxiety for Daniel, who imagines that if it, too, were to fall, it would land squarely on his room. The mysterious presence of the supernatural is also evident in the door of his room. The divisions of the four panels are disposed in such a manner as to form a Latin cross, and the inscription in gothic letters above it reads: "Souviens-toi qu'il y a dans cette pièce quelqu'un qui te voit et t'écoute en silence" (Voy, 14).

Daniel's aunt often relates old Irish legends that stimulate his natural inclination toward superstition. They combine "beaucoup de sorcellerie et beaucoup de piété" and give him nightmares (Voy, 20). The one that impresses him most particularly is the legend of Frank MacKenna, a story which intensifies the mythical dimension of *Le Voyageur*.

Frank MacKenna, forbidden by his father to hunt the hare on Sunday, disobeyed him. "Fasse le Ciel que tu ne reviennes pas en vie chez nous, si tu vas à la chasse le jour du Seigneur" (Voy, 20), cried the indignant father as Frank departed for the hunt. Frank is fey, explains Mrs. Drayton, that is to say, under the irresistible charm of death. What Mrs. Drayton does not explain is that "fey" also means "able to see into the future . . . visionary . . . marked by an otherworldly air or attitude."[4] Frank and his friends followed all day the traces of a black hare said to be of satanic origin. At dark he alone remained to pursue the hare into the mountains, where he met with a mysterious death. He was found lying dead in the middle of a circle[5] he had drawn with his stick, his hat over his eyes and his missal over his mouth. "Ainsi les paroles du père avaient été entendues" (Voy, 21).

This tale speaks eloquently to Daniel of his own situation. It reveals to him the fundamental adolescent dilemma of claustration, the irresistible temptation of escape, and his own guilt anxieties. It is the first dim prefiguration of his own fate. I observed in discussing Green's autobiography the similarity of his oedipal hallucinations to the legend of Saint Julien. Here in the legend of Frank MacKenna we find again the motif of the hunt juxtaposed with parental claustration and a weird atmosphere of demonic powers (the curse, the satanic hare). The implication is that departure for a heroic quest represented in the hunt is offered as a solution to the adolescent's immurement. An alternative answer is implied in the legend of Saint Julien, namely, renunciation or sainthood, which is itself a kind of heroic quest. This second answer is absent in Frank MacKenna's story but plays a significant role in Daniel O'Donovan's life as well as in the personal drama of Julien Green.

The call to adventure comes to Daniel from a highly unsuspected source. The eccentric old *capitaine* offers Daniel most of the funds he has and issues the challenge: "Ecoute, . . . si tu veux quitter la maison de ton oncle, je t'y aiderai" (Voy, 35). He proposes to send Daniel to the University of Fairfax.

The decision is a difficult one for Daniel. He knows that leaving his uncle's house without his permission would amount to a refusal of the financial security he has enjoyed there, for Mr. Drayton does not believe in formal education. As he ponders the problem, he wanders into the shady solitude of the Bonadventure Cemetery, where the epitaph of his now-deceased aunt seems to describe not the late Elizabeth Drayton but the psychological stage of the latent hero in Daniel: "Elle dort sous l'ombre, dans le secret des roseaux" (Voy, 28). The quiet solitude of the cemetery creates a moment of enchantment in Daniel during which he feels that he must accept the old captain's offer. At that decisive instant he sees "un promeneur qui se dirigeait de mon côté" (Voy, 38).

The appearance of the "promeneur" at the enchanted instant when Daniel decides to accept the old captain's offer enhances the portentous quality of the experience. Daniel meets him again upon his arrival at the university and feels vaguely that he has already seen him somewhere without being able to remember where. Only after having seen him several times does he realize that Paul, as his friend is called, was the "promeneur" who appeared to him in the cemetery. Paul's abrupt, unexpected appearance is usually disquieting. A vague atmosphere of mystery surrounds him, and Daniel sometimes wonders if he is really there. The epilogue of the story reveals that Daniel's friend is indeed totally a creation of his own imagination, one of the endless series of *dédoublements* in the experiences of Green's fictional characters. But despite the uneasiness that Daniel feels around his friend, Paul also inspires confidence in him. Upon meeting Paul, Daniel feels "inquiet et heureux à la fois" (Voy, 47). Daniel feels comforted in confessing to him the preoccupations of his unquiet mind, and he demonstrates an inclination to depend (often too heavily) on Paul's guidance in difficult moments. For as Virgil directs Dante's descent into the Inferno and his ascent of Purgatory, so Paul guides Daniel through the initiatory trials of his struggle for self-purification.[6]

Daniel's decision to leave his uncle's house constitutes his first step away from the claustration symbolized by the Drayton household, the first stage of his development out of the sphere of the infantile ego and into the realm of self-realization where one faces the realities of one's situation. Accepting the call to departure becomes a threshold experience, a moment of passage from one stage of development to another.[7] The significance of spiritual passage at the beginning of the initiatory stage is clear to Daniel: "Il me semblait que ma vie, ou plutôt une partie ennuyeuse et médiocre de ma vie prenait fin et qu'une autre, plus heureuse et plus active, allait commencer ce soir même" (Voy, 58).

Indeed, during the first two nights he spends at Fairfax, Daniel has a recurring dream that is a recapitulation and a deepening of the prophecy first expressed in the legend of Frank MacKenna. In the dream he sees his own self in a troubled sleep, an image recalling the aunt's epitaph. The sleeping double represents the old self that Daniel is outgrowing, the infantile ego that cannot leave the security of claustration. It is the self never fulfilling its destiny, sleeping "sous l'ombre, dans le secret des roseaux." The cry that issues from the double is an agonizing attempt to deliver the self from its suffocating immobility. It signals the dreamer-hero's departure.

Just as Daniel is leaving the reclining double, he is joined by Paul, who leads him outside into the dark night past the university, through a wood, and on a long path leading into the hills. Their feet slipping on ground still wet from an evening rain, they follow the path until they reach a plain bordering on a chasm, out of which comes an enormous roar. Fearfully, Daniel looks into the great chasm:

> Je vis de grandes eaux bouillonnantes qui se précipitaient avec violence entre deux murailles de rochers. Parfois l'eau se creusait au milieu du courant et j'apercevais un abîme d'où montaient des cris lointains, mais des vagues impétueuses le recouvraient aussitôt. Alors, j'entendis la voix de Paul qui criait: *La source des eaux-vives*! et en même temps je tombai à terre. [Voy, 62]

La source des eaux-vives (the source, or spring, of living waters or waters of life) is a biblical phrase used often to refer to the redemptive nature either of the Lord (as in Jeremiah 17:13) or of Christ (as in Revelation 7:17). In his dream, Daniel sees himself reaching the pinnacle of self-purification, the ineffable moment when the mystic is permitted to look into the vast abyss and contemplate the source of all spiritual life. It is this prophetic dream that gives spiritual meaning to Daniel's fate in reality. What may have appeared first to the citizens of Fairfax to be a demented suicide must be recognized as an authentic experience of mystical deliverance.

Finding himself once again in his room, the dreamer sees his body stretched out on the bed, but not as he had left it. Not only are his limbs broken and bloody, but his face is also different. "La figure était changée, mais d'une manière que je ne peux me résoudre à décrire" (Voy, 63). The transfiguration of the chasm experience is too extreme for Daniel to describe or understand. Again he hears his double cry out and is awakened finally from the dream.

After having repeated the dream three times, Daniel decides to escape the horror of his sleep by writing. His pen writes an account of the dream almost as if under someone else's power. With the return of day, Daniel is unable to understand what "l'autre" has written and burns it. "Est-ce que je ne m'appartiens pas? Est-ce qu'il y a une partie de moi-même qui est hors de ma portée?" (Voy, 66). It is this mysterious region of his own self to which Daniel is just beginning to awaken. The same drama was beginning to unfold within Julien Green and would develop, in *L'Autre sommeil*, into a perilous adventure of self-discovery.

Before Daniel can be permitted in reality to descend into the abyss that has been revealed only in a visionary form, he must be prepared for the fulfilment of his mystical vocation by means of a series of trials that will strengthen and purify his will. He obviously is not ready for the ultimate revelation; unable to comprehend what his dream foretells, he has burned the only tangible evidence of it.

The initiatory trials of the mystic are designed to accomplish a "purification of the self," which is "a drastic turning of the self from the unreal to the real life: a setting of her house in order, an orientation of the mind to Truth."[8] The prologue to *Le Voyageur* reports that the inscription on Daniel O'Donovan's tomb, taken from the Psalms, reads: "Comment donc un jeune homme purifiera-t-il sa voie?" (Voy, 6). Daniel's life, then, is above all a mystic's experience of self-purification.

In the course of Daniel's walk around the town of Fairfax on the day after his dream, he meets a minister with whom he has a discussion on spiritual matters. On the subject of purity, Daniel declares that je me gardais comme du feu de lire des livres hérétiques et même d'en avoir dans ma chambre, car l'impureté est en telle abomination dans la Bible qu'il me semble bien que ce soit la faute la plus difficile à remettre. [Voy, 68]

His first major trial takes place when he returns from his walk to find that Paul has taken it upon himself to burn his books and reimburse him at twenty-five cents a volume. His only possessions, the books were a vestige of the old self that highly valued what the new self considers "des livres hérétiques." By the same token, we discover shortly thereafter that Daniel has been robbed of the money the old captain had given him, and he feels certain that Paul has taken it. Surprisingly, Daniel loses no faith in his friend and asks him what he should do. After discussing the situation with him, Paul concludes that Daniel must find his way out of his difficulties on his own. Daniel is now stripped of his possessions, his financial security, and even his supernatural guide. He must stand the final test alone.

It is a moment of great illumination when Daniel sees his losses as a form of self-purification. His soul is now concentrated on the transcendental; he has proven himself worthy of the ultimate revelation:

Comment avais-je pu me tromper si longtemps et m'attacher à des livres, à mon argent, à moi-même, à ma tranquillité? La vraie tristesse n'aurait-elle pas été de se sentir la proie de tous les biens que j'avais désirés? Je fus si ému de cette espèce de révélation que je m'étendis sur mon lit pour ne pas tomber. Maintenant le monde pouvait finir et la vie se retirer de moi. Toutes les choses visibles n'existaient que pour ma tentation et par un mouvement de l'âme qui me brisa, je renonçai en un instant à la possession de toutes ces choses, à toute affection de la terre, à tout espoir de bonheur sur terre. J'eus l'impression que mon esprit se séparait alors de ma chair et que j'ètais arraché à moi-même. [Voy, 75-76]

At the apogee of self-purification, Daniel collapses in a climax of mystical ecstasy, and when he awakens he finds a note from Paul. "Il viendra quelqu'un de fort qui te prendra sous sa garde et te conduira dans tous les chemins de ta vie, si tu ne lui résistes pas" (Voy, 76). In the *Divine Comedy*, Virgil acts as Dante's supernatural guide until the threshold of Paradise is reached and there yields in favor of the guidance of Beatrice. Who is the new guide who succeeds Paul at the ultimate threshold in Daniel O'Donovan's adventure? It is his new self, guided by the purified will, which is so fully concentrated on the transcendental that it instinctively makes the right choices on its own.[9]

The letters that follow Daniel's manuscript in the form of an epilogue suggest more explicitly the anagoge of his quest. Doctor Thornton's letter describes the last few moments before Daniel left the boarding house to fulfill the prophecy of his death that had been revealed in his dream. When Daniel suddenly leaves the supper table and races into the dark, wet night, the serious-looking girl at the table declares: "Je crois qu'il est inutile de courir après lui. . . . Parce qu'il est tombé entre des mains plus puissantes que les nôtres. Il est déjà loin et vous ne le rattrapperez jamais." Doctor Thornton agrees and adds that Daniel "courait à sa perte ou à sa délivrance sans qu'aucune personne terrestre pût le détourner de son but" (Voy, 103).

The last letter reports the interpretation of the minister to whom Daniel was supposed to have spoken about "l'impureté."[10]

> Daniel O'Donovan a été . . . frappé de la grâce, mais . . . cette grâce agit souvent selon le caractère de la personne qui la reçoit. Elle convertit les doux par la persuasion, elle jette en bas les violents et les orgueilleux. Dans l'âme de ce fou elle aurait agi . . . follement, ou sagement, suivant qu'on se place au point de vue *terrestre* ou au point de vue *providentiel*. [Voy, 104]

The pattern of the quest as expressed in the dream is easily translatable into the terminology of the mystic. Through the dark night of the soul the grace of the Holy Spirit (Paul) leads Daniel out of the dark wood of perdition and up the hill of virtue to the revelation of the source of all life, the waters of spiritual regeneration, which transport him to the Heavenly City.

Imagery is not elaborate or intricate in Green's novels. The images that do recur in them are primitive and elemental, *Le Voyageur* being characteristic in this respect. The most prevalent image, that of fire, is quite appropriate to the theme of mystical development. Most of the fire images in the story are apocalyptic symbols of the refiner's fire of purification. The zealous Catholic Elizabeth Drayton burns the first written account of the dream. Paul burns Daniel's books. The fire that destroyed both the steeple of the church and the house that preceded the Draytons' is an image of divine justice that is to be feared. Daniel's landlady in Fairfax also betrays an obsessive fear of fire. The fire images of passion do not occur in *Le Voyageur* because of the undeveloped state of the erotic drama in this story.

The psychoanalytical interpretation of *Le Voyageur* is necessarily secondary to the mystical interpretation. There are, however, certain clues to Daniel's psychoerotic dilemma. The Frank MacKenna legend is evocative of the adolescent's obsessive immurement, both literally and in terms of sexual development. The father's curse represents the inhibiting forces of the family situation. Daniel's panicky fear of the church steeple that obstructs the view from his window may be interpreted as anxiety stemming from a symbol either of moral inhibitions or of the paternal phallus. The adventure prefigured in Daniel's dream is also a flight from the claustration of the parental home and a search through the frightful abyss of his subconscious for authentic sexual liberation. The tension of claustration and escape is similar in *Adrienne Mesurat* (1927), a novel of the same period as *Le Voyageur*. An interpretation that the author himself offers for *Adrienne* is equally applicable to Daniel O'Donovan's story: "*Adrienne Mesurat*, c'était moi entouré d'interdits qui me rendaient fou" (*Journal*, June 6, 1961). The "interdits" that are driving him mad are principally sexual. "Entouré" recapitulates the "cercle magique" of adolescent claustration that inhibits normal sexual development.

In making his confession to Paul, Daniel realizes that he has never suffered what he calls the mysterious temptations mentioned in the Scriptures and feels that he has missed something perhaps both desirable and frightening in his youth. "J'aurais voulu avoir des péchés humiliants à avouer et je crois que seul un respect naturel de la vérité m'empêchait d'en inventer" (Voy, 58). He senses that he is on the verge of discovering something within him that has not expressed itself, something that was necessarily suppressed for as long as he remained immured within the confines of parental dominance. Before his departure from the Drayton household, his meditative wanderings inevitably bring him to the deserted shores of the harbor, where the scene of the "petit port inactif," whose boats are anchored to immobility in the calm waters, mirrors his own cloistered state of mind. By contrast, the terrifying vision of the rocky chasm represents Daniel's first glimpses into his own fearful desires. Far-off cries emerge from the chaotic torrents but are covered over again by the waves before he can decipher their meanings.

Beneath the shadowy images, the psychoerotic drama lies still half-dormant, only partly revealed. In psychoerotic terms, the sight of the abyss is the first dim acknowledgment of the erotic dilemma, of nascent homosexuality, of repressed desire, and of sexual anxieties.

The mystic, as we have seen, is the predominant self in *Le Voyageur sur la terre*, and the sensualist remains comparatively absent. In what way is Julien Green's *moi profond* present in *Le Voyageur?* In the light of existing knowledge about the author, it may be helpful to place this *nouvelle* into the context of Green's life, taking into account both the exterior circumstances of his career as a novelist and the development of his inner nature.

Le Voyageur sur la terre was Green's *coup d'essai* in the world of French fiction. It was written during that period of his life when the discovery of the erotic side of his personality had driven him away from the Church. During the 1920s, Green was being initiated into the hard realities of his homosexual nature. The beginnings of his career as an artist coincided with this descent into the fearful subconscious desires that had been too long kept within him.

Daniel O'Donovan's adventure is a metaphorical representation of the personal quest of the author. Green is the first to admit the immense importance of the autobiographical elements in his fiction. The similarity of the young writer's quest and that of Daniel O'Donovan is no accident. The reason Daniel gives for writing his own story would be just as appropriate for Green's early career:

> Je suis dans une situation difficile et il me semble que pour en sortir je dois mettre par écrit beaucoup de choses auxquelles je n'avais pas songé jusqu'à ce jour. [Voy, 7]

These are the words of a compulsive writer, one for whom writing is the only viable therapeutic activity. Bewildered by a lack of a stable notion of selfhood, he rids himself of his obsessions through his fictional characters and only then comes to understand better his own nature.

In 1925, Green saw himself on the brink of an abyss. He was about to begin a career as a novelist, and his therapeutic method of writing entailed a search into the remotest, most frightening recesses of his subconscious. His vocation was to represent for him a Socratic quest. "Know thyself" was to be the motive behind much of his writing. Of similar significance is the inscription over the gate of the University of Fairfax: "Vous connaîtrez la vérité et la vérité vous rendra libres" (Voy, 44).[11] Paul warns Daniel of the difficulty of finding the truth. The quest for the artist is to find "ma vérité" (a term used throughout the *Journal*), the truth of what lies deepest within him.

Daniel's search is, then, a metaphorical expression of the search that Green was beginning in *Le Voyageur sur la terre*. The book is the record *par excellence* of departure in the novelist's quest for self-realization. It gives us the first partial revelation of the third self in Julien Green's personality. In immersing himself in the vocation of writer, Green was bringing himself to the great chasm of his subconscious which contained the fearful desires of a mysterious erotic nature. The descent into the raging waters of his obsessions and anxieties was a perilous one, especially for a man with the spiritual sensitivity of Julien Green. He knew that the raw material of the novelist lay essentially in the obsessions of the carnal realm. But he also knew, if only subconsciously, that only through coming to grips with the long-neglected carnal reality would he find a faith of lasting strength. For the waters of the roaring chasm into which Daniel descends represent both the chaos of sexual forces that Green was beginning to discover and the living water of regeneration that the author finds in his vocation of writer-hero. The ultimate boon of the artist's quest is what Northrop Frye calls "a fulfilment that will deliver it [the self] from the anxieties of reality but still contain that reality."[12] Such is the therapeutic effect of Green's works on his own psyche.

Frank MacKenna's pursuit of the satanic hare, Saint Julien's vocation of ascetic, Daniel's descent into the abyss of the source of living waters, Julien Green's descent into the subconscious in search of his true identity are examples of the heroic quest described by Joseph Campbell and Northrop Frye.[13] In *Le Voyageur*, Green's third self, the artist, foresees his eternally recurrent role as the hero who descends to the depths of the subconscious accompanied by a supernatural guide (Paul) and returns with a boon that offers redemption to his society (Daniel's manuscript, or the artist's final creation).

Julien Green's descent yielded his own message; it prompted Charles Moëller to call him the "témoin de l'invisible."[14] The chasm in Daniel's dream represents most fully "that abyss to which the descending consciousness submerges in dream, where the individual life is on the point of dissolving into undifferentiated energy . . . the perpetual life-giving, form-building powers of the universal source."[15] The fearful obsessions that he was to explore turned out to be "la source des eaux-vives." The perilous descent was indeed a "victory of fertility over the wasteland."[16] It was a descent that he had only begun with *Le Voyageur sur la terre*, and the artist's quest would be renewed with the beginning of each new novel or play. The ultimate test would cause death as in Daniel's case only in the sense that death is a deliverance, a rebirth. It was the search in the dark regions of the fictional realm, peopled with his anxieties and desires, that enabled Green to realize his third self. The very act of writing afforded him the opportunity to be reborn into the life that he was destined to create for himself.

Chapter Three

Self-Discovery in *L'Autre sommeil*

The publication of *L'Autre sommeil* in 1931 marked a significant development in Julien Green's writing career. After much worry and inner turmoil, Green had finally brought himself to treat the subject that was the most terrifying to him, the problem of homosexuality. Gide, who had liked *Le Voyageur sur la terre*, had encouraged Green to be as open and frank as possible on sexual inversion in his writings. Despite Gide's complaint that *L'Autre sommeil* would be regarded as the story of a Platonic love rather than an authentically homosexual experience, the book was an important step away from Green's characteristic reticence. Although treated with a delicate touch, the theme of homosexual desire in *L'Autre sommeil* carries the same emotional intensity that one encounters in the most candid personal revelations of his recent autobiography.

L'Autre sommeil recounts the discovery in a young man of his own erotic nature. Denis is presented in the first pages as an adolescent dominated by fear and solitude. Imprisoned in a family situation that inspires only the feeling of alienation, he has no firm notion of his identity. He has only negative ideas about his selfhood, seeking to set up barriers between himself and his parents and loathing any resemblance he might have to them. He fears the impatience of his father and feels only coldness toward his mother. Their deaths represent for him a kind of deliverance, a severing of his ties with an unwanted past. For Denis, solitude brings the freedom to realize a new existence and a new identity. The main events in his life amount to a series of revelations that lead him to a full recognition of his erotic nature. They are presented in a crescendo of emotional pressure that is matched only in the second principal work Green wrote on homosexuality, *Sud* (1953).

The opening scene of the novel introduces eight-year-old Denis and the future object of his desires, his thirteen-year-old cousin Claude, in a situation that combines many of the essential elements of Denis's story. Claude is holding Denis on top of the parapet of the pont d'Iéna by the ankles. Denis's accustomed sentiment of fear thus appears in the context of a precocious form of sadism, an important aspect of Green's erotic fantasies. It is significant also that one of the sights that impresses itself on Denis is that of "la blanche nudité des statues qui dominent le fleuve" (AS, 3). Classical sculpture—which incorporates nudity and immortality—plays an analogous role in Denis's homosexual awakening to that which it served in the erotic fantasies of the hero of *Mille chemins ouverts* and *Terre lointaine*.

The fact that Denis's parents disapprove of Claude's crude, rustic ways lends him the seductive attraction of the rebel in his young cousin's eyes. Denis admires his robust strength and what he calls a "coquetterie du désordre" (AS, 16)—tousled hair and unbuttoned shirt. But the first indication of the direction in which Denis is developing is the scene in which he contemplates Claude in a deep sleep on the first morning of their vacation in Chanteloup. His strength mirrored in the plenitude of sleep, Claude's rounded arms lie above his head.[1] The sheet wound around one of his legs is creased and folded in the same manner as the drapings that the Greek sculptors first moistened and then arranged on the limbs of their models. Denis's first homosexual experiences, latent though they be, are associated with the beauty of Greek sculpture. The ideal of transcendent physical beauty as expressed in the Greek statues is evocative of the Platonic reveries of adolescent innocence. Denis does not know what is going on inside him, and so he can be lyrical or melancholy about Claude's beauty without feeling consciously abnormal. The importance of sculpture in the development of sexual inversion is a major motif not only in *L'Autre sommeil* but also in *Moïra*, *Chaque homme dans sa nuit*, and the autobiography.

The first overt revelation of Denis's nature comes two years after his father's death. It occurs at the period of his adolescence that he calls a second birth, that is, the awakening of undifferentiated libidinous energy within him. "L'homme naquit en moi dans des larmes d'angoisse" (AS, 72). A recurring dream at this stage of his development is just as prophetic to Denis as Daniel O'Donovan's dream was in *Le Voyageur*.

In the dream Denis sees a very large room flooded with warm air and light. Except for a monumental bed, the room is bare. There is a magical noise entering the open window. It sounds like heavy hammers being banged on iron beams at a distant construction site, but for the dreamer, "Quelqu'un venu des régions inhumaines faisait entendre la voix géante du destin" (AS, 75). Indeed, the content of the dream is a prophecy of Denis's destiny. Two nude bodies lie asleep and perfectly immobile on the bed, only the tips of their fingers touching. Their robust limbs and "respiration heureuse" recall the picture of the sleeping Claude. There is no trace of fear, suffering, or any unpleasant emotion on their faces, for they represent to the dreamer the image of perfect joy untainted by sorrow. The climax of the dream comes when in a moment of tumultuous emotion, Denis identifies both of the sleeping bodies as himself. "Ce rêve m'instruisit mieux sur ma vraie nature que toutes les méditations et tous les gestes dictés par mon désir. Je sus que j'étais voué aux sens" (AS, 77).

Not long after his dream, Denis happens to visit a sculpture shop that gives him his second major identity revelation. After several visits, he asks if there are any other works besides the busts he has examined there. He is led to a dark storage room that houses the larger statues of the gallery. Contemplating the miniature Olympus alone, he is devastated by the spectacle of the beauty of the mythological deities. They are at once the incarnations of his desires and the mirrors of his solitude.

Les visions incertaines de mes rêves prenaient corps et pendant l'espace de quelques secondes je me connus exactement, quitte à oublier par la suite ce que cette révélation m'apprenait. . . . Chacun vivait d'une passion qui n'échauffait que lui. [AS, 86, 84]

In a paroxysm of desire, Denis touches the statues with trembling hands, caresses and embraces their majestic bodies. He is astounded that the haughty-looking gods consent to his caresses, and he wonders at the defenselessness of these models of ideal beauty.

The next revealing experience for Denis is the first incident in which real life and his dreams begin to meet. An ugly classmate named Remy, who takes pleasure in manipulating the emotions of his friends, invites Denis to join him and his cousin Andrée on an excursion to the country. Andrée is actually Remy's mistress, a stunningly beautiful girl totally at the mercy of the brutal Remy. The boy uses Denis's presence to humiliate Andrée and uses her as bait with which to tantalize Denis's erotic fantasies. "Tu as envie d'elle? . . . Elle est belle, n'est-ce pas? . . . Elle m'obéit" (AS, 97-98). In order to save Andrée further humiliation, Denis leaves the apartment, but in the stairway[2] outside he is overcome by the turbulent desires and anxieties within him. Seated on the stairs, the vision that comes to him is first one of complete darkness, then a kind of flash in the obscurity, and finally the image of the two bodies on the other side of the door, coming together in terror and joy.

Andrée soon writes a note to Denis, appealing for his help in relieving her of the sadistic treatment she suffers at the hands of Remy. Their meeting is the revelatory incident in this erotic triangle. It occurs to Denis that his idea of beauty is intimately related to that of strength. Andrée, however, displays the opposite characteristic, going to great lengths to humiliate herself in his eyes. She loses all the angelic attractiveness that he thought he saw in her at first. In attempting to discuss their relationship, Denis comes to the astounding discovery that his violent jealousy is directed not toward Remy but Andrée. Remy's ugliness attracts him more profoundly than Andrée's beauty, and his closeness to her is really only a means of approaching Remy.

Green's analysis of the germination of an imperious passion in Denis offers the most profound observations of his early career on love and desire. When he meticulously points out all the illogical manifestations of jealousy in Denis's three-way relationship with Andrée and Remy, one is reminded of the very similar study of erotic strategy in Proust's story of Marcel, Albertine, and the various suspected third parties. There are scenes in both novels in which the protagonist relentlessly badgers his beloved for confessions of the infidelities that he imagines her to have committed:

> Chaque réponse que j'obtenais me procurait une souffrance nouvelle, mais j'en jouissais comme du plus rare des plaisirs. . . . Je revivais maintenant les pénibles moments que j'avais passés, l'autre jour, dans l'escalier, mais transformés en je ne sais quelles amères délices. [AS, 115]

The fundamental difference, of course, lies in the fact that Remy turns out to be the beloved in *L'Autre sommeil*. Moreover, a passage such as the following recalls vividly the Proustian doctrine of the "intermittences du coeur."

> Rien de mystérieux comme le cheminement d'une passion dans un coeur sans expérience. Elle semble parfois se perdre et disparaître, mais une fatalité le mène et sa route est sûre. [AS, 117]

Denis's high expectations for his meeting with Andrée having ended in disillusionment, he realizes that his desires lie beyond Andrée and the traditional heterosexual experience she represents. At this point he feels nostalgia for the erotic world represented by the statues in the sculpture shop. "Au seuil du monde inexploré rayonnaient les statues des dieux. . . . Elles se portaient garantes à mes yeux d'une vie semée de prodigieux plaisirs" (AS, 118). The image of Remy also represents a whole world of desires and sorrow that is pursuing him.

Denis's definitive discovery of his erotic nature comes on the night after his mother's death. He finds an old family photograph album and destroys all the pictures of his parents, in accordance with his desire to escape their influence and find his own destiny. The only photograph that he saves is one of Claude, who has been in the war and has not seen Denis in years. As he is going to bed, he is informed that Claude has returned to Paris and will be at his mother's funeral the next day. Alone in his room he takes out the picture of Claude and ponders it once again. "Ce fut comme si ma vie jusqu'à ce jour n'avait été qu'une longue et lente ascension vers la minute que je vivais maintenant" (AS, 165). He feels that all the remaining years of his life will be marked by his actions. At that moment, all of the suppressed desires that have been hesitating inside him are released, and he places a fervent kiss on the image of Claude's face.

This scene is the climax of Denis's adventure in self-discovery. It liberates him from the adolescent self that was totally dependent on the family for its identity, and it enslaves him to a new self that is not totally acceptable to society. The last two scenes that bring the two cousins together are poignant studies of unrequited passion. Denis feels compelled to confess his love to Claude but knows it is impossible. During their final idyllic reunion at Chanteloup, he has one more opportunity to witness the spectacle of his cousin lying in a deep sleep. The surging of the pulse in Claude's neck reminds Denis of the two sleeping bodies of his dream. Denis's last amorous act is as mysterious as the rest of his story. He kneels over and causes his shadow to pass across Claude's cheeks and mouth in a strange kind of noncorporeal touching.

Those are the salient moments of discovery in Denis's erotic development. They trace the awakening of homosexuality in the protagonist. But *L'Autre sommeil* is not simply a novel on sexual inversion, and Denis is not simply a homosexual hero. We have already mentioned the importance of his search for identity. "Une seule chose me guidait: je désirais passionnément me connaître" (AS, 120). Let us not assume that the acknowledgment of his erotic nature marks the end of his Socratic quest. As Jacques Petit has noted, *L'Autre sommeil* and *Epaves* are exceptions among Green's novels in that they are open-ended.[3] Green's novels often end in some form of catastrophe: death, insanity, or crime. In *L'Autre sommeil* and *Epaves*, we leave the protagonist with much of his life ahead of him. In the case of Denis, the aspects of the story other than homosexuality that I shall now examine encourage the reader to admit a unique potential for development that is made possible by *L'Autre sommeil*'s open-endedness.

Sexual inversion is the most obvious, but not the only means by which Denis seeks to deny his past, to find deliverance in a new existence, to "devenir autre." The sculpture shop and the dream of the two sleeping bodies are not only revelations of an erotic nature. They afford access to another world radically different from the one that Denis longs to leave. The plastic beauty of sculpture connotes an ethereal kind of love, and the ubiquitous motif of sleep (in the dream, in the moments when Denis contemplates Claude) approximates the unworldly stillness of the statues' beauty. The erotic development of the sexual invert remains as the central intrigue on which *L'Autre sommeil* is structured, but it is related to a development on a mystical level for Denis. The transformations of the Greenian self are richly varied in this novel, in which the problem of identity begins to emerge as one of the author's major preoccupations and evolves on three planes that correspond to the erotic, mystical, and artistic aspects of Julien Green's personality.

Denis chooses very carefully the places where he attempts to leave his existential situation for another reality of his own choosing. He especially prefers those places where life appears in an unreal aspect, seeking to find the intermediary state between dream and reality. The sculpture shop is the first *lieu d'élection* that he frequents. The supernatural beauty of Greek gods frozen in time transports Denis into a nontemporal region where he is free to explore the unknown aspects of his personality. Another favorite point of epiphany is an old, abandoned construction site near the Champ-de-Mars. The work has been stopped at the precise point where the framework offers just enough outline to suggest a form while not being too neatly finished to allow the free rein of one's imagination. The unfinished nature of the building lends an atmosphere conducive to discovering mystical aspects of everyday existence.

Cet espace devient le lieu d'élection où la vie se transforme. [AS, 127]

Une espèce d'opération magique donnait à mes rêves le poids des choses réelles, et les souffrances qui m'avaient déchiré le coeur semblaient à présent des cauchemars dont je m'éveillais. J'échappais enfin à la vie. . . . Il y avait . . . une zone de silence où j'étais seul et libre. [AS, 130]

In his dream of the two sleeping bodies, Denis imagined the spacious room to be on the top floor of a building near the Champ-de-Mars, and he said that the hammering noise that he called the voice of destiny must have been coming from a nearby construction site. So the abandoned, unfinished building figures implicitly in the dream before it appears explicitly in the narrative and is related to the theme of destiny.

The nocturnal dreams and the waking reveries that take place in the *lieux d'élection* are concerned with Denis's discovery of homosexuality. They may also be interpreted, however, as part of his initiation into the meaning of death. The mystic can interpret everyday life only through the perspective of death and its implications. The meaning of death is one of the most important problems for a mystic to ponder, and he is always sensitive to revelations of death's significance. For Denis, one of the first intuitive experiences of death involves his sense of smell. As a young child, Denis is enchanted by the scent of rain-soaked, decomposing leaves in the garden of the Passy apartment, an odor that he calls "une haleine de mort" (AS, 8). In the last scene with Claude at Chanteloup the same smell intoxicates him as "le parfum d'une existence nouvelle" (AS, 183). The development of Denis's mystical awareness is evident in these two passages. He has begun to understand death not as a terminal point, but as a passage from one form of existence into another.

The olfactory dimension of Denis's acute sensibility is sharply delineated in *L'Autre sommeil*. Many of the images evoked by smells in this book are reminiscent of Baudelaire's doctrine of correspondence. The bittersweet nostalgia for childhood innocence and aspirations in Denis is touched off by his awareness of the spiritual content in an evocative fragrance.[4]

Aujourd'hui encore, lorsque je passe par certaines rues, une ou deux fois l'an, si l'air est frais, s'il a ce quelque chose de virginal que l'on sent aux approches de l'automne, j'entends les appels de mon enfance. Tout recule et s'efface dans la nuit de la conscience; il n'y a plus que ces voix indistinctes que je suis seul à écouter.[AS, 8-9]

The aspiration to escape "anywhere out of the world" is also connected to a particular smell: "le parfum d'une existence nouvelle." Denis is a kind of Baudelairean mystic, as are many of Green's heroes. Like Baudelaire's *mauvais moine*, he glorifies death and is obsessed by the claustration of his own mind and by the sin of spiritual sloth.

The night after his mother's death, Denis lies in his bed thinking of his mother's corpse on the bed in the next room. He compares mentally the relentless decomposition already beginning to take its toll on her and his own pulsing, vibrant body, in which so much libidinous energy is only beginning to come to life. The bed is the locus of richly ambivalent meanings. Here Denis contemplates the supernatural stillness of sleep. Here he has dreams that take him to a mystical world. And this scene contrasts the death bed to the bed that holds the flower of youth, the life force itself.

Denis's contemplations of death become the most revealing aspect of his spiritual experience. At his mother's funeral it is he who has requested a mass to be sung. Even though he professes to be unreligious, the familiar words of the *Dies irae* work on him almost unconsciously and the beautiful *prosa*, or text, of the mass proclaims to him the existence of an invisible universe. During the service, the painful impossibility of his desires for Claude leads him to wish ardently for death to take him in an absolute form of deliverance from himself. Again, the mystical aspiration to escape takes over.

The last scene of the book marks the climax of Denis's mystical initiation into the meaning of death. At the end of his reunion with Claude at Chanteloup, Denis is able for the first time to think of his own death as a real and inevitable event. Even with his beloved cousin near him on a beautiful, sunny summer day, everything around him is, ironically, speaking to him only of the end of all life.

Thus, the apparent story of homosexual development betrays a mystical dimension; yet the mystical dimension does not necessarily overshadow the analysis of erotic passion in Denis. The eros intrigue is, rather, an essential thematic corollary to the mystical and artistic aspects of the Greenian protagonist illustrated in Denis.

A novel with a quotation from Pascal as a rubric could hardly be totally concerned with the theme of sexual inversion. The title of the book comes from a passage in *Les Pensées* in which Pascal compares and contrasts the ultimate reality of the waking state with the state of sleeping.

Qui sait si cette autre moitié de la vie où nous pensons veiller n'est pas un autre sommeil un peu différent du premier, dont nous nous éveillons quand nous pensons dormir?[5]

The mystic regards exterior reality as a dream that obscures the ultimate reality of the spirit. Sleep offers him a radically different perspective from which to interpret life. Denis declares that he can only believe in something when he has dreamed it. Hence the great importance to him of dreams as prophecy. In the abandoned building site, he has a vision of his dead parents that finally renders the fact of their deaths real to him. It is a revelation of an already accomplished fact by means of hallucination.

An important element of the dream of the two sleeping bodies is the identification of both bodies as Denis. The phenomenon of *dédoublement*, already strikingly present in *Le Voyageur sur la terre*, again is involved in the strange transformations of the self. The dreamer sees himself as two persons simultaneously; he discovers that there are at least two identities developing within him, the eroticist being initiated into sexual inversion and the mystic uncovering the spiritual reality to which he awakens from "the other sleep."

Denis recalls several instances of the same kind of mystical experience we find in the young Julien of *Partir avant le jour*. Particular moments remain indelible in the youth's mind—"la merveilleuse immobilité des choses autour de soi" (AS, 9)—as he sits motionless on the floor of his room holding his breath, frightened by the silence and the thickening shadows of the oncoming night. Once again the stillness that characterized sculpture and sleeping figures signals the advent of the spiritual order. It is this same immutable stillness that gives art a kind of immortality, once it fixes within a stable form the idea or experience that will live long after the death of its creator. Denis's first day at the vacation retreat in Chanteloup is filled with the violent pleasure of simply existing. He rolls on the grassy slopes, laughing without reason, giving vent to an excess of happiness. When the vacation is cut short by his father's death, he lies face down on the banks of the Seine and closes his eyes, concentrating his attention on the fragrance of the earth. Remaining motionless for several minutes, he reaches a near hallucinatory stage in which he experiences vertigo and the sensation of falling. The mystical flight from an all too painful exterior reality is momentarily accomplished.

The role of the dreamer is the one in which Denis illustrates in all its complexity the divided personality of Julien Green. Denis's dreams foreshadow his later homosexual development, and they usher him into the passage from the world of exterior reality to the spiritual realm. Moreover, they offer a deepening of the conception of the artist in Green's fictional universe.

A dream such as the one that confirms for Denis the reality of his parents' deaths has a remarkable effect on him.

Le pouvoir d'hallucination est si fort chez moi que la chose imaginée cesse de paraître telle, pour peu que je m'abandonne à son prestige, et revêt toutes les apparences de la matière. Dans un cas semblable, toucher ce que je vois n'ajouterait rien à mon illusion, qui est parfaite. [AS, 149]

For the writer who is the witness of a vision, writing is never cut-and-dried, prestructured, or even controllable. He is the instrument of a magic process in which two realities communicate. For this reason the eroticist and the mystic coexist in Green's fiction; they are the inseparable antagonists of the basic conflict that produces the third self.

The greatest gift for the artist, according to Green, is "cette espèce de vue intérieure dont la force me distingue des autres hommes, ce regard aigu et avide" (AS, 152).

Ce don de voir . . . cette faculté particulière de voir par les yeux de la chair ce que d'autres se représentent faiblement par l'esprit. [AS, 149-50]

It is this visionary quality of the artist that becomes increasingly important in the middle part of Green's career as a novelist. *Minuit* and *Le Visionnaire* are notable examples of the theme.

In the *Journal*, the author himself has expressed eloquently the importance of the visionary aspect in his writing.

J'écris ce que je vois. S'il fallait me résumer moi-même en tant qu'écrivain, je crois que cette phrase dirait à peu près tout. Si je ne vois pas, je ne puis écrire, je veux dire que si je n'ai pas devant les yeux de l'esprit une représentation très nette de la scène que je veux décrire, et je dis bien une représentation, comme on dit une représentation théâtrale, je ne puis rien faire. . . . Il y a en moi quelqu'un ou quelque chose qui me fait voir mes personnages et me les fait voir en train d'agir. [J, 785]

In discussing the autobiography, I noted the immense importance of the visual image in the erotic development of the young Julien. Now we begin to appreciate equally the significance of the visionary image for Green the artist. Eminently important to the genesis of his fictional writings is the visionary process of which he speaks in the *Journal*.[6]

In the October 16, 1949, entry of the *Journal* from which the preceding passage was taken, Green says the visionary quality was at a peak during the composition of his first three novels, somewhat weak in *Epaves*, and strong again in *Minuit* and *Le Visionnaire. Varouna* and *Si j'étais vous* were almost totally lacking in visionary content, whereas *Moïra*, which he was writing at the time of the entry, was revealed almost entirely in a single vision that came to him with the dawn of one morning in 1949. The novels that Green lists as having been created by means of the *seconde vue* are the ones in which the third self, the *moi profond*, is most fully liberated and best expressed.

Chapter Four

Escape and Deliverance in *Le Visionnaire* and *Minuit*

Le Visionnaire (1934) and *Minuit* (1936) explore in depth the motive of escape in Julien Green's fiction. *Minuit* was actually begun first and set aside temporarily for the writing of *Le Visionnaire*, which Green finished in late 1933. In fact, Green reveals in the *Journal* (p. 121) that he sometimes alternated his work on the two novels during 1933. In both novels the author permits himself to become increasingly engrossed in the realm of the fantastic. Jacques Maritain was disturbed by the preponderance of the dream world in *Le Visionnaire* and may have sensed the dangerous direction that his friend's exploration of the supernatural was beginning to follow. For in 1934 Green had begun a serious study of Buddhism, which by September of 1935 had helped him come to grips with his obsessive fear of death. Monsieur Edme of *Minuit* is a guru who preaches doctrines of oriental mysticism. Green's fantasy world, thus influenced by oriental mysticism, was to lead him even further in the fictional motif of escape with *Varouna* (1940) and *Si j'étais vous* (1947). These two novels show that Maritain's apprehensions were partly justified. They tend to rely too heavily on exoticism and fantasy, and Green himself, as we have noted, admits that they mark the low ebb of the visionary's *don de voir*. In *Le Visionnaire* and *Minuit*, however, the protagonists' *grandes évasions* are described with the authenticity of things seen, and they give us a more intimate look at the author's third self.

Manuel, the *visionnaire*, and Elisabeth (of *Minuit*) are victims of the prolonged adolescent claustration that haunts so many of Green's fictional characters. In each case, the development of the novel traces a desperate struggle for deliverance that ultimately leads to death, the most beautiful of the exotic *pays lointains*. Both have the sensitivity of a mystic in that everyday life seems less and less real to them. They aspire to mystical escape in the revelations of night, of dreams, and of death. And their indulged fantasies lead them both to mysterious castles where life is transformed. At the same time, their struggles for deliverance have an erotic dimension. Each seeks to overcome basic sexual insecurity and traditional prohibitions in order to achieve sexual fulfillment. The erotic and spiritual elements are masterfully interwoven in the struggles of these protagonists.

The image of the castle, so similar in these two novels, has several possible meanings. Green has suggested that Fontfroide in *Minuit* is the symbol of the soul. The powers of spirituality and sensuality are represented by M. Edme and Serge respectively, and their struggle to win over the soul forms the essential action of the novel. But the castle may also be interpreted as an image of death. In the novels that precede *Le Visionnaire* there are several examples of ominous houses that harbor the protagonists' superstitions and fears. *Mont-Cinère*—one of the more obvious examples—, the Villa des Charmes in *Adrienne Mesurat*, Daniel's uncle's house in *Le Voyageur*, and Ferrières in *Les Clefs de la mort* are *ébauches* of the castle of death, which finds its most complete delineation in *Minuit* and *Le Visionnaire*.

Death is an unkown entity that both terrifies and attracts the Greenian hero. In the earlier fiction there are allusions to its horror and its inscrutability, but it is never directly confronted. *Minuit* and *Le Visionnaire* are an exorcising of the obsession with death, symbolizing Green's deepening spirituality and his study of oriental mysticism. But they are also a means by which Green has dealt with the obsessions, perhaps as efficacious a means as the new spirituality that they symbolize in real life for Green. He has always approached his problems in two ways: through religious faith and through his vocation of visionary artist. Thus, his novels are not only emblems of his psychological and spiritual struggles but also a means of dealing with them.

Manuel in *Le Visionnaire* is a disillusioned young man who has abandoned earlier intentions to join the priesthood. His adolescence was a time of great spiritual fervor in which he was very studious, strove to achieve saintly perfection, and remained totally chaste. By the time of the story, he has lost his faith and suffers from the persistent role of future priest that people continue to impose on him. He has become an advocate of Renan, and his readings of *La Vie de Jésus* have led him to consider Christ the incarnation of revolt. The image of Jesus the rebel is the one with which he identifies when he finds himself frustrated by his own inept timidity and impotence.

Manuel, like Daniel O'Donovan and like Elisabeth in *Minuit*, is orphaned and has been taken into a relative's home. His case is singular in that Mme Plasse, the aunt who becomes his guardian, was in love with Manuel's father and has spent her life in bitter resentment at having lost her lover to her sister. The widowed Mme Plasse loves Manuel both as a son and as the reincarnation of his father. But her love is an overprotective, domineering kind of passion that is never fully requited. Likewise, Manuel suffers because of his desires for Mme Plasse's daughter, Marie-Thérèse, who does not love him in return.

Because of her role as narrator, the character of Marie-Thérèse is presented in depth. Green employed the technique of multiple narration in *Le Visionnaire* by placing Manuel's *récit* within the framework of a two-part narration by Marie-Thérèse that opens and terminates the novel. Part One serves mainly to delineate the situation at Mme Plasse's house, but Marie-Thérèse also tells her own story with particular attention to the details of her spiritual development. At the Catholic school she attends as a young girl, she has a brief experience of precocious piety, and she tells her mother she wants to pursue a religious vocation. Mme Plasse is quite severe in her disapproval of the idea: "Apprends, ma fille, qu'une catholique sérieuse n'a pas de visions" (Vis, 40). The spiritual reveries of the young girl have been partly a means of escape from the cold austerity of her mother's house. Her deepest wish is for deliverance: "Si j'étais libre" (Vis, 48).

The first experience in which Manuel's influence on Marie-Thérèse is evident is, appropriately, a kind of escape. In the middle of the night, Marie-Thérèse awakens and stands at her window contemplating the night, which begins to work a powerful spell on her. The real world is gradually replaced by the strangely different realm of night, and Marie-Thérèse begins to feel a kind of liberation from her ordinary existence.

> Il me sembla que j'allais découvrir l'aspect secret des choses, celui qu'on entrevoit en rêve . . . et en même temps je me sentis envahie d'une immense tendresse; oui, je baissai les paupières et tendis la bouche à la nuit, au vent qui passait sur ma face. [Vis, 50]

Obeying a sudden impulse created by the moment of enchantment, Marie-Thérèse removes her nightgown and looks at her bare body with the intoxicating pleasure of transgression. Brimming with her newly found sensuality, she lies on the carpet and rolls "comme un jeune animal qui dépense ses forces" (Vis, 51).

At that moment she recognizes the sound of Manuel's footsteps pacing in the dining room directly beneath her room. She quickly dresses and goes down to join him. Manuel leads her to a mysterious enclosed meadow called "l'Hermitage," which recalls the *lieux d'élection* of *L'Autre sommeil*. In the middle of the night the glow of moonlight intensifies the eerie atmosphere of l'Hermitage. Here Manuel reveals to Marie-Thérèse that his suffering is caused by the desires she inspires in him. The scene is the culmination of Marie-Thérèse's discovery of sensuality. When Manuel caresses her legs with his cheek she faints, and the swoon is strangely associated in her mind with the idea of deliverance. Caught in the claustration of stifling moral and physical restraints, the adolescent Marie-Thérèse has discovered two ways out. The spiritual escape of monasticism has been cynically squelched by her mother. The discovery of her own sensuality gives her only a fleeting hope for sexual liberation with Manuel. Still, her relationship with Manuel will prove to be her only opportunity for deliverance until she is permitted to leave home, but the escape will not be sexual. To Marie-Thérèse, Manuel represents something deeper than sexual liberation and quite apart from religious escape; he offers her a radical flight from the weight of existence into a unique visionary realm.

Marie-Thérèse's predilection for reverie makes her readily receptive to the charisma of Manuel's profoundest nature. A rosary that she keeps long after her childhood spiritual aspirations retains the qualities of a fetish for her in a way that recalls the suggestive power of smells in *L'Autre sommeil*.

L'odeur de ces grains de bois jaune était si forte qu'il me suffisait de la respirer pour faire revivre en moi certaines minutes de mon enfance, non les gestes, ni les paroles, mais la qualité particulière d'un moment. . . . Il ne s'agissait plus de souvenir, mais de la renaissance d'un monde disparu, avec sa lumière, son souffle, ses rêveries fugitives. Même athée, je me retrempais dans cet élément merveilleux qu'on appelle la foi. [Vis, 65]

While Marie Thérèse is dissatisfied with her life, Manuel is pathologically oppressed by the anguish of his existence. He, Daniel O'Donovan, and Elisabeth of *Minuit* have much in common with Oedipus and Hamlet. They are orphaned wanderers who are searching for their parents and whose destiny is the certainty of death that weighs heavily on their lives. Their search is also a quest within, an attempt to know their profoundest nature, and they reflect Green's continuing identity search, the movement toward self-discovery that characterizes all of his works.

Manuel is beset with the problem of claustration both at work and in Mme Plasse's house. Of a sickly constitution, he is mercilessly exploited by his employer at the bookstore until he is finally forced to quit his job because of his failing health.

Manuel's existence in Mme Plasse's house is equally a kind of immurement. Every aspect of life is regulated by his aunt's austere schedule, and it is nearly impossible to escape her domination. "Tout plaisir, en effet, lui paraissait suspect" (Vis, 2). The most serious crisis of his sickness, however, brings a significant change to the situation. Mme Plasse has a pronounced predilection for misfortune and has come to enjoy in a perverted sense the role of mourning that has befallen her with the successive deaths of her sister, her husband, and Manuel's father. The invalid, especially the doomed invalid that she discovers Manuel to be, enjoys a particular prestige in her house. By a certain disposition of her nature, Mme Plasse feels "un élan vers tout ce qui est chétif ou blessé" (Vis, 71). She devotes all of her time and energies to the care of her nephew. She expresses her concern in religious terms, but Marie-Thérèse cannot help seeing in her mother's devotion a love of a less celestial nature. In a photograph of the two from the time of his convalescence she sees Mme Plasse in a different role.

Malgré sa robe et son voile noirs, ma mère semblait respirer la joie orgueilleuse de l'amour. . . . Cette femme dont le coeur dormait depuis si longtemps connut le réveil d'une passion toute humaine. [Vis, 71-72]

In his own narration, Manuel himself reveals the classically oedipal aspect of the situation. While he is recovering from the attack his aunt pampers him. On warm days, she sits next to him and sings as she rocks the hammock for him. "Une paix délicieuse tombait sur moi" (Vis, 126). Here the claustration of Mme Plasse's house offers security and peace. The warm comfort of the maternal figure could not be more oedipal. But Manuel cannot find lasting peace with the morbid, voracious Mme Plasse.

Manuel is typical of Green's heroes in that his motivations are confusingly divided between the spiritual and the erotic. When Mme Plasse repeatedly refers to her daughter as "ce grand corps bête," he is obsessed by the image of his cousin's nude body, which imposes itself on his mind irresistibly. When Marie-Thérèse is forced by her confessor to reveal the incident at l'Hermitage, Manuel reflects on the bitter irony of being accused of promiscuity after having led such a pious youth, obsessed with the goal of purity. The prolonged sexual chastity and innocence of his devout adolescence have a significant effect on his sexual life as a young man. "L'image d'une femme éveillait en moi une sorte de folie et me faisait peur" (Vis, 150).

Despite his loss of traditional religious faith, Manuel betrays a latent mystical tendency that has not been stifled by his spiritual difficulties. Lying awake in his bed just before dawn, he suddenly feels the presence of someone standing near him: "Lui peut-être," he thinks.

> Ce fut alors, je le crois, j'en suis sûr, que sur mon front une main se posa, d'une fraîcheur délicieuse, brûlante. [Vis, 130]

The means of escape from the claustration of Mme Plasse's house begins as a game between Marie-Thérèse and Manuel, "le jeu du château." The castle actually exists in the novel, but the characters only get a fleeting distant glimpse of it through the trees when they ride in the carriage through the countryside. Manuel begins to invent tales about fictitious inhabitants of the place, and his fantasy world soon captures Marie-Thérèse's imagination. The two cousins, and especially Manuel, begin to participate in a new hallucinatory existence, "un monde à la fois violent et poétique, éclairé d'une lumière plus impérieuse que la nôtre" (Vis, 5).

In revealing this strange world to Marie-Thérèse, Manuel is the most complete fictional incarnation of the visionary role of the third Greenian self. In this sense, *Le Visionnaire* may be considered a portrait of the artist as visionary. The transformation that occurs in Manuel when he leaves everyday life for his imaginary existence in the château de Nègreterre is analogous to the transformation of the self when Julien Green writes his novels and plays. In real life Manuel is a weak-willed, insignificant person, but his visionary self is altogether different, as Marie-Thérèse tells us:

> Il rencontrait à tout moment . . . le doute de soi et la peur de mourir, mais ici, dans un univers à l'image de sa nature secrète, profond, terrible et radieux, il jetait le fardeau de la vie réelle et retrouvait sa vraie stature. [Vis, 5]

The analogy between the visionary Manuel and Julien Green is still deeper, as reflected in Manuel's description of the manner in which he sees his visions. "La nuit, en effet, alors que tout notre être semble à la limite de deux mondes, un peu avant la seconde où j'allais tomber dans un grand sommeil vide, je *voyais*" (Vis, 153). The quotation recalls the visionary process that Green himself undergoes in writing his novels.[1] The invasion of the visionary reality occurs for Manuel, or for Julien Green, only when he is relaxed and passive, detached from the exterior world. The Greenian third self, the visionary artist, exists on the threshold of two realities—"à la limite de deux mondes"—and plays the role of witness. Never inventing the action, he simply records what he sees taking place in the autonomous fictional universe.

In Green's fiction there is a continuous interplay of sensual and spiritual forces that we see illustrated in Manuel and Marie-Thérèse. The corresponding duality in the author adds depth to the conflict, and the great relief that the protagonists feel in escaping to Nègreterre is indicative of the degree to which Green's therapeutic writing has been essential to his stability and his very survival.

When Marie-Thérèse is sent to live at a boarding school and Manuel can no longer share with her the "jeu du château," he begins keeping a journal in which he records not only the details of his drab life with Mme Plasse, but also his imaginary experiences at Nègreterre. Manuel's journal, like Green's, is an exercise in self-discovery. The syndrome of the compulsive writer is apparent in Manuel's confessions.

> Quatre ou cinq mots jetés sur une page blanche que je déchire aussitôt ont suffi quelquefois à me rendre courage dans une heure d'incertitude. En écrivant, me semblait-il, je respirais mieux. [Vis, 218]

The last part of Manuel's narration is entitled "Ce qui aurait pu être," and it is an account of his imaginary adventures at the château de Nègreterre as they appear in his diary. With Marie-Thérèse away at boarding school, he is left in the house alone with Mme Plasse, who grants him the tranquility to indulge his obsessive need to write. Thus, Manuel becomes entirely immersed in the imaginary world he has created. The period in which he writes "Ce qui aurait pu être" is the last days of his life, and Green has called his experiences at the château "une sorte d'apprentissage de la mort" (J, 92).

The château de Nègreterre, in Manuel's account, is inhabited by the noblest and most eccentric family in the area. The patriarch of the family is an old count who has been on the verge of death for years. His daughter the viscountess and his son Antoine have been profoundly affected by their father's obsession with death. In a remote tower of the castle he has cloistered himself in near-complete isolation. Being alone with Monsieur de Nègreterre gives Manuel an opportunity to acquaint himself with death in all its terrifying immediacy. The count seems already to have left reality and to be at the threshold of another world. In reading the Church Latin aloud to him, Manuel feels that his life in the castle is fulfilling his destiny, a fate presided over by a higher will to which he is more sensitive than other people. This intimacy and responsiveness to a strange power that guides his life are major aspects of Manuel's role of visionary.

Antoine de Nègreterre, son of the count, is haunted with the fear of succumbing to the same mysterious illness that has plagued his father. His reaction to the call of death, instead of stoic preparation, is a furious determination to experience all of life's pleasures, illicit or not. The two scenes in which he meets Manuel reveal the latent power that death has come to exert on him behind his hedonistic pose. In the first scene, Manuel by chance encounters Antoine and his sister in the garden. Without warning or explanation, Antoine strikes Manuel, sending him reeling to the ground, and warns him not even to pronounce his name. The viscountess later warns Manuel to avoid her brother, and Manuel knows her brother's reputation for brutality. However, Manuel one afternoon unfortunately comes upon Antoine once again. The young aristocrat insults Manuel and shows complete scorn for his weakness. He then offers Manuel a chance to avenge the humiliation he suffered in their first encounter. Dismounting from his horse, Antoine orders Manuel to choose a good stone and to throw it at him. The sadomasochism of the scene foreshadows the duel of *Sud* (1953), in which Ian challenges the man he secretly loves and lets him kill him. Both Antoine and Ian ask for punishment and death after they have made others suffer. When Manuel fails to hurt his enemy, Antoine remounts and lashes his riding crop[2] across Manuel's face as he rides disdainfully away. As in *L'Autre sommeil* and later in *Sud*, sadomasochism is integrally related to the homosexual tendencies of Green's heroes.

Manuel's relationship with the mistress of the castle sheds light on his latent sexual inversion and bears comparison with the scenes between Manuel and Antoine. The viscountess is a domineering young woman who insults Manuel almost as cruelly as her brother does. Her imperious attitude toward Manuel keeps him in a servile position during his entire stay at Nègreterre. But despite the abuse and humiliation he suffers at her hands, he is intrigued by the way in which she has been captivated by the mystical charm of death. Like Frank MacKenna, the viscountess is incurably fey.

Both Manuel and the viscountess express a fundamentally ambivalent feeling toward the castle. Life at Nègreterre is fraught with tension and anxiety and the castle is compared to a prison, but they are attracted to Nègreterre by the irresistible fascination of death. Death has the same ambivalent aspects for Julien Green. It is seductive because of the peace, rest, and security—in a word, escape—that it offers. But at the same time, the threat of eternal punishment gives it a chilling hostility.

On two different occasions the viscountess reveals to Manuel the morbid fantasies that have entranced her for so long. Death appears to her in the form of images that suggest the ultimately ineffable reality. When asked why she remains at Nègreterre, she replies:

> Je veux savoir comment cela finit, la vie, oui, de quelle manière on entre dans la mort. C'est plus fort que moi. Il y a là quelque chose qui m'attire et me tient. [Vis, 243]

This cult of death as a mystical reality that teaches the hidden significance of life is the force that binds all the characters to the château de Nègreterre. Green originally intended to divide "Ce qui aurait pu être" into chapters, the most intriguing of which was to be entitled "*Ars bene moriendi.*" In this part, which in the definitive version describes the inhabitants of the castle, he says he intended to depict "des personnages qui s'efforcent de s'élever au niveau de la mort, et la mort comme un magnifique soleil noir" (J, 91-92).

The fascination of Green and his heroes with the dead is an important motif that reflects their mystical sensibility. Commenting on the death of Pierre Meyer in 1933, Green writes of the impression he has of the dead.

> On dirait que, moralement, les êtres changent en mourant et grandissent. Ils deviennent d'une manière indéfinissable, nos aînés, sans doute parce qu'ils *savent*. [J, 106]

The great catastrophe of Green's youth gave him the first intuition of the strange knowledge to which the dead are privileged. When he entered the room to be alone with his dead mother for the last time, the fourteen-year-old Julien witnessed the same mystery.

Elle était devenue quelqu'un de majestueux comme une reine, séparée de moi par de grands espaces, absorbée dans une méditation qui demeurait secrète. [PAJ, 224]

In *Sodome et Gomorrhe*, the deaths of Marcel's grandmother and Albertine, after the process of *l'oubli* and involuntary recall, come to enhance their importance in his mind. The "culte du regret pour nos morts" teaches Marcel of the significance of his departed loved ones in his life.[3] In Green's novels, the dead teach the heroes of the new life upon which they are embarked, a transcendent, mystical reality that does not appear in Proust's novel. The intensity with which Green the visionary describes that realm persuades us that he has long lived in unusual intimacy with the reality of death.

The viscountess's obsession with death eventually reaches a hallucinatory point. She tells Manuel that she has come to regard life as an illusion and death as the only authentic reality. The world for her is a mirage, nothingness, meaninglessness. Because she senses intuitively that Manuel understands her feelings about death, the viscountess is compelled to reveal them to him. But even though he acts as her confessor, Manuel still detects the condescending manner of her abuse in the midst of her confessions. It is as though she is speaking only to herself.

The denouement of "Ce qui aurait pu être" and of Manuel's narration is one of the most fascinating moments of Green's fiction. It reaches a degree of erotic intensity unprecedented in Julien Green's writing. Shortly before dawn of Manuel's last night at the castle, he is awakened by the viscountess, who enters his room and announces that her father is finally dead. The act of making love that follows a few minutes later is accompanied by and confused with disgust and hatred in Manuel's mind. It is at once a means of gratifying his frustrated desires and avenging the humiliation that the viscountess has made him suffer. But Manuel's role has never been anything but passive in his relationships with others, and the love scene is no exception.

Le corps pâle et froid de ma maîtresse se refermait lentement sur le mien, pareil à ces fleurs monstrueuses dont on dit qu'elles emprisonnent l'insecte qu'attire la douceur de leur parfum. . . . Au plus fort de la volupté, j'eus l'impression de me débattre et de réchauffer une morte dont l'inflexible étreinte ne se desserrerait pas. Cet enlacement glacial me fit savourer la terreur au coeur même du plaisir et ce qu'on appelle l'ivresse des sens ne m'empêcha point de comprendre que j'étais la proie et non le maître.[Vis, 251-52]

The reversal of roles in the sex act is another indication of Manuel's extreme passivity. In all of life, even in the culmination of his imaginary adventures at Nègreterre, he is always the possessed and never the possessor. The association of love and death observed earlier in *L'Autre sommeil* becomes quite obvious in this scene, for the viscountess dies just seconds after Manuel succeeds in freeing himself from her embrace. The sexual fulfillment that Manuel has long searched for is only another form of claustration (the "enlacement glacial" of the embrace) from which he must again escape. On the other hand, the viscountess finds the ultimate escape in death.

The continuation of Marie-Thérèse's narration recounts the death of Manuel. During a vacation from boarding school, she leads him out of the house and away from town to a place where they can see the château in the distance. There Manuel succumbs to a final attack of his illness and dies in her arms, saying: "C'est presque du bonheur" (Vis, 270). Erotically, his life ends in failure. Spiritually, as in the case of Daniel O'Donovan, his fate may be interpreted in various ways, but not with certainty. His death does, we know, deliver him from the anxieties of a painful existence and lead him to the reality to which his mystical self has aspired. But the visionary aspect of Manuel's personality is the most successful role he plays, and it leads us to a deeper understanding of Green's third self.

Manuel's closest spiritual relative among Green's protagonists is also his closest contemporary, namely, Elisabeth of *Minuit*. We have already noted some of the similarities of these two characters, mainly that they are orphans who are received in someone else's home and whose lifelong search for escape or deliverance leads them to a castle and finally to death. Elisabeth's search is more involved than Manuel's. The succession of homes that she either flees or is forced to leave is a more explicit recapitulation of Oedipus's wandering search for his parents. Her complicated itinerary finally leads her to the house of her stepfather, a device reminiscent of Dickens' melodramatic recognition scenes. Ironically, she dies without recognizing her relationship to Monsieur Edme.

On the day when her mother (Blanche) kills herself, Elisabeth's aunt, Marie Ladouet, comes to take her from school and hides the truth of the suicide from her. Elisabeth, however, senses what has happened. Her fear expresses itself in a strange way.

> Il lui semblait, en effet, qu'une main la tenait à la gorge et serrait de temps en temps; alors le sang lui montait à la tête et elle craignait de tomber. [Min, 26]

The terror of death thus is expressed in an image of strangulation, another form of the "cercle magique" of Green's claustrophobic protagonists, and in the fear of falling.

When the news of Blanche's death is finally revealed to Elisabeth, Marie Ladouet tries to soften the blow by offering a gift, an old pair of scissors. An argument ensues, and the wretched aunt tries to retrieve her begrudged gift, but Elisabeth uses the scissors to defend herself and makes a large tear in Marie Ladouet's dress. Later, when Elisabeth goes to pay her last respects to her mother, she takes out her scissors, cuts off a lock of Blanche's hair, and puts it in her pocket. The cutting of the scissors sounds sinister to her.

The cruelty of Marie Ladouet encourages Elisabeth to escape from her house, but she finds no refuge with a second aunt. At Rose's house, Elisabeth realizes that she has been committed to the care of a deranged woman. Rose is too lost in her own obsessions (she washes the kitchen floor all night, imagining that her dead husband has soiled it) to give her niece a supper or a decent bed. After Elisabeth is shut up in her room, she has a frightening initiation into the world of night. A brief sleep is troubled by a dream that reveals her fundamental anxieties. She imagines herself being carried in a prone position as in a kind of procession that leads to a church. A long black box is also brought. One of the most striking impressions she has is that of the absolute immobility of her body. She is vehemently chastised by the people gathered in the sanctuary, and suddenly the vault of the nave splits open loudly as an enormous mass of water crashes into the church from the black sky. At that moment she realizes that it is she who is in the coffin, "son étroite prison de bois" (Min, 44). Before the dream, Elisabeth was kept awake by her panicky fear of the dark. She has a feeling similar to "la lente suffocation d'une noyade" (Min, 39), an image not unlike the first one associated with death—strangulation and falling. The little room has an oppressive atmosphere that recapitulates the image of claustrophobia, and Elisabeth finally escapes through the window.

Elisabeth's ensuing nocturnal wandering is a ritual initiation into the unreal world of night. It recalls Marie-Thérèse's midnight scene in her bedroom and at l'Hermitage with Manuel. The sexual awakening of Elisabeth is appropriately less advanced because of her age, but there is the same erotic impulsiveness produced by the unaccustomed atmosphere of night. She approaches a square with a bronze fountain in the middle, dominated by the statue of a nude woman with butterfly-like wings on her back. Alone in the dark square, Elisabeth is free to enjoy the delicious sensation of watching what she has been told is "improper." She walks around the fountain and gazes at the nude woman, "tout heureuse de frôler le mal, puisque le mal c'était d'être nue avec des ailes de papillon dans le dos" (Min, 47).

The atmosphere of night during Elisabeth's wandering through the dark town recreates the same kind of enchantment that Denis found in his *lieux d'élection*. The whole world is mysteriously transformed by the extraordinary silence and the strange light.

> Pendant plusieurs secondes elle éprouva quelque chose d'analogue aux enchantements des vieux récits, car de crainte de rompre le silence elle ne remuait pas, et plus son immobilité se prolongeait plus il lui paraissait difficile d'en sortir. [Min, 48]

Elisabeth's natural inclination to reverie is reflected in the piano lesson scene of Part Two. As Elisabeth's instructor plays a waltz for her, she drifts off into a dream in which amorous aspirations are juxtaposed with the macabre atmosphere of a graveyard. Elisabeth interprets the setting as the garden of her childhood. Her reverie reintroduces the persistent double image of love and death.

The most remarkable incident in Part Two, which recounts Elisabeth's life with the Lerat family, is the *rémouleur* (knife grinder) scene. The image of the scissors reappears here with increased suggestiveness. It recurs in conjunction with one of Elisabeth's flights from the claustration of the adolescent within the family, just as it did when she used the scissors as a weapon in escaping Marie Ladouet. But in this case it is explicitly linked with an abortive escape that is described in sexual terms. The knife grinder is a robustly attractive young man who has the same kind of appeal for Elisabeth that Serge will have later in the narrative.

Elizabeth is gazing out the window of the Lerat house into the street at the beginning of the scene. She is the adolescent who dreams of deliverance from the tedium of family life; the window is the image of access to a more exciting reality. When the grinder passes by, she has a sudden, irresistible impulse to take her old scissors to him. "Depuis un moment, il lui paraissait indispensable de les faire aiguiser" (Min, 86). She embarks on a long labyrinthine chase of the grinder through the most frightening streets of the town. Throughout the scene, Elisabeth is urged on by something stronger than her own will. Like Manuel, she is impelled in her quest for deliverance by the force of destiny, to which she is especially responsive. She finally finds the grinder's cart but does not succeed in having him sharpen the scissors. The scene ends with Elisabeth looking through a smoke-filled café at the grinder. The unformed impulse to deliverance that is represented by the scissors and Elisabeth's sensual attraction to the knife grinder thus end in frustration. For the moment she is forced to return to the life of claustration within the family. The failure of the escape foreshadows the fatality to which her quest as a whole is doomed.

Jamais plus qu'à cette minute elle n'avait si durement senti les contraintes où se brisaient chaque jour les élans d'un coeur naïf, et des larmes roulèrent sur ses joues. [Min, 90]

The strange higher will that impells her to escape from the Lerat house—at least momentarily—is destiny. And the particular aspect of life with the Lerat family that she is trying to escape is "les contraintes" that are oppressive to her adolescent dreams and aspirations.

The mysterious force of destiny, or fate, that shapes the development of this scene is the clue to the significance of the scissors image. In Greek mythology, the three Fates[4] were the infernal divinities who presided over the spinning of man's destiny. Clotho, the goddess of birth, spins the thread of life; Lachesis determines its length; and Atropos is in charge of cutting the thread of life. For Elisabeth, the scissors are at once a means of severing ties with an unwanted past—of cutting the umbilical cord of adolescent claustration—and a constant reminder of the weight of fatality with which she must live. Her successive escapes will ultimately lead her to the final *évasion* of cutting life's thread.

The importance of fate in *Minuit* is typical of its significance in the whole of Green's fictional universe. The identity quest of his heroes is closely related to the search for their destiny. The culmination of the intrigue is usually susceptible to two interpretations, as in *Le Voyageur*. Death can mean victory, through the eyes of the mystic, or it can mean tragedy. Whatever the final interpretation, the atmosphere of tragedy in the world of Green's fiction is reminiscent of Greek tragedy (e.g., his three plays: *Sud, L'Ennemi,* and *L'Ombre*). The fate against which the protagonist struggles is crushing in its ineluctability. In a profound sense, Green may be considered a novelist of the human condition. What makes his novels different from those of a Malraux or a Sartre is that tragedy for Green does not preclude two more answers to man's fate: His fiction suggests the possibility of transcending death through mysticism or through the vocation of the visionary artist.

Part Two of *Minuit* ends with the death of Elisabeth's adoptive father, an event that necessitates her moving to Fontfroide. Before she is ever told of M. Lerat's death, she has a chilling presentiment of it. "Elle devinait la grande présence invisible qui envahissait la maison, et ses mains se glaçèrent" (Min, 102).

In Part Three, Elisabeth arrives at the castle of Fontfroide. The old structure was once a convent, and the façade of the house still shows the trace of the cross that once hung over the entrance. M. Edme has bought it as a retreat, a place of meditation, and he has received all the less fortunate members of his family in the household. Elisabeth's introduction to Fontfroide brings many frightening experiences. Climbing the stairs to her room with M. Edme's servant Agnel, Elisabeth hears one stair creak with the sound of a whip.[5] The first night at Fontfroide, she dreams that someone is watching her sleep. She soon discovers that all the inhabitants of Fontfroide follow M. Edme's regimen of sleeping during daylight and spending their waking hours during darkness. M. Edme believes in and reveres the mystical value of darkness, as opposed to light.

Elisabeth's nocturnal explorations of the household result in some rather unusual encounters. In one room she finds a woman and her daughter sitting patiently in their traveling clothes and watching the clock on the wall. The woman indicates that they are awaiting the hour of departure of a train that will take them away from Fontfroide forever. Elisabeth later learns that the woman and child wait in the same room every night for the mythical one o'clock train. Similarly, Elisabeth, having been warned by one of the inhabitants to leave Fontfroide, is able only to reach the garden outside the house, where she feels a strange force holding her prisoner to the castle. Like Manuel, she wants to escape but cannot. The eternal waiting of the woman and her child is a metaphor charged with metaphysical connotations. They are in a sense waiting for Godot. Elisabeth, too, is similar to Beckett's "clochards" in the end of her scene in the garden.

"Il faut que je m'en aille, se dit-elle à plusieurs reprises, sans bouger. J'irai jusqu'au village, je demanderai qu'on m'indique la mairie."
Elle rentra. [Min, 164]

In the final scene of *En Attendant Godot*, Vladimir suggests, "Alors, on y va?" and Estragon replies, "Allons-y," but the pair remain motionless as the curtain drops.

Elisabeth's most dramatic and most fateful encounter in the castle of Fontfroide is her discovery of a young man named Serge. In one of the rooms of the castle that she explores in total darkness, she hears someone's rhythmic breathing. Concluding that it is the respiration of someone sleeping in an armchair, she strikes a match in order to look at him.

The light of the burning match reveals a captivating spectacle for Elisabeth: "Un garçon, d'environ dix-sept ans dormait dans une de ces attitudes à la fois tragiques et nonchalantes par lesquelles le sommeil s'apparente à la mort" (Min, 173). Elisabeth has never seen anyone as beautiful as the sleeping boy. Like the sleeping figures Denis contemplates in his dream in *L'Autre sommeil*, the immobility and serenity of sleep lend Serge a special kind of attraction. Green specifically compares Serge's slumping posture to that of death, recapitulating the tragic nature of love and desire in Green's fictional reality. Elisabeth's reaction to this awakening of her desires is characteristically ambivalent. She is exhilarated by the possibility of fulfillment in love, but she senses instinctively the ultimate deception of desire.

A présent elle n'aurait su dire si c'était la joie, une joie inquiète et déchirante, ou la plus étrange et la plus exquise douleur qui la faisait trembler ainsi. [Min, 173]

When Serge awakens, he promises Elisabeth that they will escape Fontfroide together. But first he must assist Agnel in serving the customary midnight meal at which M. Edme presides. Elisabeth hides in a storage room and witnesses the scene. When M. Edme arrives, he has the servants light all the candles and proceeds to exhort his followers in a monologue of prophetic visions. He berates the alarm that financial ruin has caused in them. He reminds them that in former prosperity he warned of trusting too much in an illusory reality. If they, like him, had cultivated "le goût de l'invisible," the desire to possess would have vanished and they would now be in what he calls "cette indifférence bienheureuse," confident that what they fear does not really exist.

In the course of his exhortation, M. Edme recounts a dream he had long ago that revealed to him the existence of the castle of Fontfroide. In the dream he was wandering in the countryside when the miraculous appearance of Fontfroide made him wonder whether it was imaginary, even though he could feel the walls with his hands. In the midst of a feeling of complete temporal disorientation, the presence of the castle is comforting and protective. The security it offers is expressed in images recalling the protectiveness of the maternal influence. "Il semblait que la grande maison me protégeât, qu'elle étendît sur moi son ombre comme une aile" (Min, 214). In real life Green was looking to the Church for this same kind of security, and his fictional counterpart M. Edme envisions Fontfroide as an ideal dwelling that will offer security in the ultimate *évasion*, the escape of the spirit to a mystical reality.

In order to convince himself of Fontfroide's reality, Edme must, in his dream, pass a self-imposed trial. Realizing that the seemingly imaginary castle is built over the dark waters of a sinister-looking swamp, he knows that passing the threshold will determine unequivocally the reality or unreality of Fontfroide. If it is an empty vision, his first step will plunge him into the sinister swamp. As in so many other instances in Green's fiction, the atmosphere of medieval romance has taken hold of the narrative. In visionary form, Edme is expressing a great moment of transition in his life, a threshold experience *par excellence*. The perilous step of faith into a mystical reality represented by Fontfroide is what is demanded of Edme, a passage from one world into another. He responds affirmatively and feels great exaltation when his foot encounters the hard stone floor of the castle. Inside he experiences a marvellous transformation. "Plus aucun désir ne m'agitait. Le doute, les regrets, la tristesse me quittèrent, et cette incertitude de ce que nous sommes" (Min, 216). Fontfroide, explains Edme, is a symbol of the ultimate refuge, the deliverance that can only be attained in the "forteresse de l'âme."

Tout est ailleurs, mes amis, tout ce qui est vrai est ailleurs. [Min, 218]

This evocation of a mystical realm that radically transcends exterior reality demonstrates that Edme is not only a guru of oriental mysticism. He also represents Julien Green's conception of the visionary artist, a conception that draws on a tradition of angelism whose greatest exponent was Rimbaud. Edme's teachings are strikingly similar to certain statements in *Une Saison en enfer*, for example. "La vraie vie est absente. Nous ne sommes pas au monde" (*Délires*, I). It might be observed in this connection that a cinematic adaptation of *Si j'étais vous*, in which Green collaborated with Eric Jourdan in 1954, was retitled *Je est un autre*, a famous quotation from Rimbaud's *Lettre du voyant*. The visionary artist, or *voyant*, is the third self that participates in a mystical reality which Edme's angelism evokes.

Edme's speech has a hypnotic effect on Elisabeth. Intuitively he knows the power of his words. "Dans le plus rebelle de vous il y a un dormeur qui obéit à ma voix" (Min, 225). The *dormeur* within Elisabeth is entranced by his visionary teachings. When Serge returns to take her away, she refuses. "Je veux rester ici. . . . Je serai plus heureuse à Fontfroide avec M. Edme" (Min, 227). Serge, however, storms his way past Edme and the others with Elisabeth and manages to lock himself and Elisabeth in an isolated room of the castle. There the young girl comes out of her trance, and Serge makes love to her. When Edme and his friends find them, Serge shoots Agnel in order to escape with Elisabeth. The two are pursued as far as Elisabeth's room, where they try to escape through the window. Both lose their footing and fall to their deaths.

In the *Journal*, Green says that Serge is the incarnation of physical desire and M. Edme that of the desire for spiritual things (J, 615). At the end of *Minuit*, Elisabeth is forced to choose between Serge and Edme. Despite her wish to follow Edme's mystical way, Serge compells her to choose the gratification of her physical desires. The agony of the conflict is another expression of the violent struggle between the erotic and the spiritual forces in Julien Green.

Elisabeth's death is described in terms that recapitulate the themes of fatality and deliverance that were suggested earlier in the novel. When she begins climbing out of the window, she feels an alien force pulling her away to the void.

> Le gouffre l'appelait, car elle appartenait au gouffre. . . . Et maintenant, de sa grande voix silencieuse il lui parlait déjà le langage secret que seuls comprennent les morts. [Min, 239]

But her death is not just tragic destiny, for as she is falling she sees Agnel walking serenely across the sky toward her, his face shining with a luminous joy. ''Avec un sourire d'une bonté sublime, le vieil innocent lui tend les mains et elle se sent soulevée de terre par une force irrésistible'' (Min, 239).

Manuel of *Le Visionnaire* and Elisabeth of *Minuit* are participants in the characteristically Greenian quest for self-discovery. Both are impelled by an irresistible force toward one of three possible ends: fatality, escape, or deliverance. The castles they discover finally take on the significance of principal characters in the stories. They hold mysterious powers of enchantment over their inhabitants, and they are the *lieux d'élection* where the Greenian visionaries (Manuel and Edme) discover a mystical reality.

Chapter Five

The Violence of the South: *Moïra* and *Sud*

The period of Julien Green's career following *Minuit* was dominated by two important events that occured in 1939: Germany's invasion of France and Green's reconversion to the Catholic faith. He was obliged to spend the duration of World War II in the United States, and despite his American citizenship, the humiliation of France and the loss of his whole way of life in Paris caused him the grief that was suffered by all true Frenchmen at the time. The writing he did during his wartime "exile" reflects how gravely he was shaken by the course of world events. He was able to finish *Varouna* (1940), begin *Le Malfaiteur* (finished only in 1956), and write *Memories of Happy Days* (1942) and *Si j'étais vous* (1947), but none of these books ranks among Green's most compelling works. The most notable exception in this relatively infertile period is the *Journal*, whose importance seems to have been enhanced by the author's spiritual development. It is clear from the *Journal* of the 1940s that Green was in a stage of grave questioning. Would a wholehearted reconversion undermine the spontaneity of his artistic creations? How could he reconcile the two vocations of novelist and Christian?

By 1950, however, a whole new stage in Green's career unfolded with the publication of *Moïra*, which signalled the full maturity of the novelist's talent. It is significant that with this novel Green returned to the American South, the setting of his turbulent college years, a setting that had been so successful in two works of his youth (*Mont-Cinère* and *Le Voyageur sur la terre*) and was to be pursued with equal success in works of his maturity (*Sud, Chaque homme dans sa nuit*, and *Terre lointaine*). Robert de Saint-Jean suggests that *Moïra* represents a kind of "nouvelle vague du Sud."[1] While the South is not the only setting of *Chaque homme dans sa nuit*,[2] *Moïra* and *Sud* are two powerful evocations of the South whose differences and similarities blend to create a strong impression of the significance of the land of Green's ancestors in his own personal drama.

Moïra is highly autobiographical and compares favorably with certain parts of *Terre lointaine*. The source of the novel is the young writer's experience at the University of Virginia, and the action takes place in 1920. Green's life as a student at Virginia serves, however, only as a point of departure for the story of Joseph Day.

The action of *Sud* is not autobiographical. *Sud* is a historical play in that it recreates an era, the antebellum South, and dramatizes the problems of that historical moment. But the psychological implications of these problems for the main characters are extremely important in understanding the three Greenian selves in a nonhistorical perspective.

In these two works, the spiritual aspects of the writer's personality are involved in his most complete fictional portrayal of the obsessive world of complex erotic strategies. The conflict of erotic and spiritual forces creates the violent agon that makes both *Moïra* and *Sud* such powerful examples of tragedy.

The atmosphere of these two works may be described most characteristically as violent, and Joseph Day, the protagonist of *Moïra*, is first and foremost a creature of violence. His thick red hair is the most visible symbol of his inflammatory temperament. Having grown up in an isolated mountain community, he arrives a the university with an acute awareness of being different from the other students. His primitive religious background has given him a fanatical intolerance in matters of sex. He is shocked that his landlady uses makeup, smokes cigarettes, and does not reserve her piano for sacred music on Sunday, as was the practice in his home. He overhears classmates in the boardinghouse discussing with great zest the sexual encounters that inevitably occur in college life. Because of his religious background and extreme sexual innocence, he considers them to be in the very clutches of perdition.

> Ici même, dans cette ville de la plaine qu'est notre Université, des milliers d'âmes sont en péril du feu éternel. Dieu veut qu'on les avertisse. S'il le faut, je leur parlerai, moi. Je monterai sur une chaise et je leur parlerai de l'Enfer. [*Moïra*, 207]

Joseph feels compelled to save the souls of those whom he encounters at the university. He believes that every one he meets has been sent to him by God to be saved. The great mission of his life, which constantly preoccupies him, is "sauver des âmes." Because of his extreme emotional naïveté, Joseph regards others only as souls to be saved and cannot relate to them as flesh-and-blood people. This missionary zeal and puritanical fixation on the abstraction known as the soul have tragic consequences, once Joseph finds himself involved in complex relationships with others.

The fundamental violence of Joseph's psychological nature is expressed in radically ambivalent terms. The image of fire, for example, is rampant in the novel in various contexts. Green refers to the book in his *Journal* as the "Roman du Roux" (J, 625), and Joseph's hair is termed "cette chevelure de flamme" (*Moïra*, 1). The action takes place in autumn, when the trees display "ces tons d'incendie" (*Moïra*, 7), and in the sky "le crépuscule jetait des couleurs d'incendie" (*Moïra*, 171). Joseph's second landlady, like Daniel O'Donovan's, anxiously asks him whether he smokes, explaining that she has a terrible fear of fire. In the scene of Joseph's sexual consummation with Moïra, the overturned lamp from under the bed casts a weird light on the ceiling that resembles the glow of a fire. And "le feu éternel" of infernal punishment is an image that Joseph constantly invokes.

In an inspired moment with his friend David, Joseph speaks eloquently of his violent nature.

Tu aimes le Seigneur dans la paix, mais moi, j'ai la rage de Dieu. Je ne puis aimer qu'avec violence parce que je suis un homme de désir. C'est pour cela que je suis plus exposé à perdre la grâce et que d'une certaine manière je suis plus près de l'enfer que tu ne le seras jamais. Tu ne sais pas ce que c'est que l'enfer, mais moi je le sais, parce que je sais ce que c'est que le feu. Le feu est ma patrie. [*Moïra*, 207-08]

The wrath of divine punishment is expressed for Joseph in terms of fire. His love of God is of a fiery nature. But the absence of God is also a kind of fire: "du feu noir" (*Moïra*, 208). One is reminded of the firebrand theology of Théophile Delaporte, the pseudonym under which the young Green published the violent "Phamphlet contre les catholiques de France" in 1924.

The same violence characterizes Joseph's long-dormant libidinal impulse, which asserts itself against his will in a devastating struggle. Throughout his life at the university he is constantly beset with obsessions of a sexual nature. The preoccupations with love in Shakespeare, and certain risqué allusions, lead Joseph to drop the modern literature course in favor of Chaucer, whom he discovers to be equally obscene. He finds *Romeo and Juliet* boring because, never having been in love, he considers a man's passion for a fourteen-year-old girl supremely unimportant. What interests him is the salvation of souls, and the souls of these two lovers are assuredly suffering in hell now for having thought only of satisfying their passions. The statues of Apollo and Hermes that stand outside one of his classrooms are impure because of their nudity, and Joseph carefully avoids looking at them.

Like Denis in *L'Autre sommeil* and Wilfred in *Chaque homme dans sa nuit*, Joseph is strongly affected by the plastic beauty of the human body in sculpture. These three heroes reenact the drama of the young boy of *Partir avant le jour*, whose Calvinist concept of nudity could not be reconciled with the fact that in the Louvre he saw nudity glorified on pedestals.

One of the most remarkable things about Joseph Day is that in spite of his sexual innocence and ignorance, he seems to have a power of attraction for almost everybody he meets. Three relationships reveal the peculiarities of his erotic nature.

His friendship with Simon, who boards in the same house, reveals Joseph's astounding sexual ignorance. Simon is so solicitous of Joseph's companionship that he becomes a pest. An aspiring young artist, he tries to make Joseph appreciate the beauty of the bodies of Apollo and Hermes, whom Joseph regards with disgust because they are naked idols. Later, he succeeds in coaxing Joseph to permit him to draw a sketch of him. When a classmate discovers the picture, he mockingly laughs at Joseph's profile, which Simon has embellished with the eyelashes of a movie star. The nature of Simon's attraction to Joseph becomes evident to all but Joseph, whose fierce religious convictions lead many to believe he has no base passions. He returns to his room one night to find a magnolia blossom on his desk with a note that reads: "Moins blanche que toi" (*Moïra*, 64). He chastises Simon for what he considers a joke, the real significance of which he simply cannot understand. Simon tries to explain discreetly to Joseph how he is suffering, but Joseph's reply is always "Je ne comprends rien à cette histoire" (*Moïra*, 81). Joseph's inhumanity toward Simon leads the latter to warn him prophetically that in spite of his coldness, "Toi aussi, tu souffriras, un jour. Tu verras ce que c'est!" (*Moïra*, 83). Because of Joseph's tragic lack of human understanding he is concerned only with whether Simon, like the others, is endangering his soul by frequenting the local brothels. "Je me demande s'il est sauvé" (*Moïra*, 84). Two days later, he learns that Simon has killed himself.

The first erotic relationship of the novel in which Joseph's own emotions become involved is a mysterious, ambivalent one that develops implicitly with another student, Bruce Praileau. If Joseph's sexuality is latent, his homosexual tendencies are even less conscious. Praileau makes fun of Joseph's red hair in front of some other students, and the incident leads to a fight. Praileau's look of derision makes Joseph want to punish him for his pride. But in the midst of the ensuing fight Joseph discovers a new impulse within himself.

Subitement, une joie folle l'envahit à se sentir si fort et il eut l'impression d'assouvir une faim mystérieuse. [*Moïra*, 29]

At the end of the fight, Bruce tells him they must never again speak to each other for a reason that he cannot reveal. What he does divulge is another prophetic warning of Joseph's tragic ending: "Tu es un assassin. . . . Il y a en toi un assassin" (*Moïra*, 31). Joseph has no further dealing with Praileau until the end of the novel, but his image obsesses Joseph throughout the narrative. He never fully discovers the nature of the obsession, but it is involved always with the themes of sadomasochistic punishment that are prevalent in *Moïra*. In one sense, the more fully delineated relationship of Ian and Erik in *Sud* is the sequel to the drama of sexual inversion that is only outlined in *Moïra*.

In fighting Bruce Praileau, Joseph is both punishing him for his pride and satisfying his own subconscious erotic drive. Immediately after the incident he wanders off into the forest and succumbs to a delirium of rage. The frustrated desires within him that he can neither understand nor admit make him cry out in anguish. Picking up a limb from the ground, he beats the trunk of a sycamore with it. His arms seem to function of themselves, while a falling leaf brushes his cheek like a hand caressing him. After a moment he faints into a deep sleep. The next morning he has to leave the classroom and go to the restroom for a fit of nausea. "C'était de rage qu'il était malade . . . c'était d'une honte mortelle qu'il avait vomi" (*Moïra*, 43). The devastating struggle of repressed erotic forces and spiritual aspirations makes him literally ill.

The punishment theme plays an important role in Joseph Day's ideas, as we have seen with the images of fire. David Laird, Joseph's friend who is a preseminary student, tries to tone down his rigid morality, telling him he must learn to understand human frailty and fight the devil with whatever weapons God gives him. "Avec un fouet, comme Jésus dans le temple" (*Moïra*, 96), exclaims Joseph, invoking the powerful Greenian image of sadomasochistic punishment.

Twice in the novel, the stair in Mrs. Dare's house cracks under Joseph's step with the sound of a whip: first, when he approaches for the first time the room he will occupy (*Moïra*, 3), and second, when, after moving to Mrs. Ferguson's house to avoid his neighbor's lewd conversations, he returns to retrieve a forgotten sweater. He finds the room occupied by Moïra, who humiliates him and arouses his desire to punish her.

The image of the stair appears once again in a moment of deep anxiety. Joseph is passing into a mode of reality hitherto unknown to him. He knows subconsciously that he is being initiated into the second Greenian reality, namely, the realm of erotic forces whose nature is indicated by the image of the whip that is conjured up by the sound of the stair under his foot. The symbol of the erotic reality, of course, is Moïra, whose room he is approaching in both passages.

Bruce Praileau is introduced in a scene at the dinner table of Mrs. Dare's boardinghouse. When he leaves, the porch door slams with the sound of a gun. For days after their fight, the scene retraces itself in Joseph's mind with obsessive persistence, particularly "cette voix qui semblait lui couper la figure comme un fouet" (*Moïra*, 41).

Frank MacAllister, another boarder at Mrs. Dare's, taunts Joseph with sarcastic allusions to his own activities with the local prostitutes. When his suggestive gestures become too blatant for Joseph's sense of decorum, *l'ange exterminateur*—as Joseph begins to be called—flies into another tantrum of rage and whips MacAllister across the back with his belt. Afterwards, an inner voice tells Joseph that it is not MacAllister whom he wishes to punish, but Praileau.

The third and most important erotic relationship in which Joseph becomes involved is his passion and hatred for Moïra and for what she represents. The significance of the character of Moïra is, indeed, an enigma in the novel. It is curious that the title should be taken from the name of a character who first appears on page 156 of a 251-page novel. The adopted daughter of Mrs. Dare, she is the woman of dubious origin. Mrs. Dare's letter to her suggests that Moïra may be of mixed blood.

Tu viens on ne sait d'où. Je te conseille de ne pas faire voir tes mains en plein jour: elles te trahiraient. Tes ongles surtout. J'ai mon idée là-dessus. [*Moïra*, 35]

The author himself states in the *Journal* that the original version of the novel that became *Moïra* was "l'histoire d'une mulâtresse" (J, 723).

Moïra's principal role in the action of the novel is that of the temptress. Killigrew warns Joseph that she is what the Latins call a *lupa*, a she-wolf, "une bête sans cesse affamée. . . . Elle se donnerait à un gorille" (*Moïra*, 175). For two reasons she considers it a personal challenge to seduce Joseph, to conquer his apparent cold angelism: because she is insulted that Joseph has not pursued her, and because she has agreed to help MacAllister and his friends play a trick on *l'ange exterminateur* by making him lose his virginity. Her conduct toward Joseph is always intensely provocative, especially in her final scene with him.[3]

Moïra's significance, however, is hardly confined to the role of mulatto temptress. The author's foreword points out that Moïra was one of the Greek names for destiny or fate. Long before her actual appearance on the scene, there are numerous allusions to her that foreshadow the tragic conclusion of Joseph's story which she precipitates. When Joseph enters his room at Mrs. Dare's in the opening scene, he notices a cigarette box that Mrs. Dare identifies as belonging to Moïra, who ordinarily occupies the room. On one Sunday while the Negro maid is cleaning the room, she mentions the fact that Moïra was particular about keeping the bed in a certain position and remarks casually, "Elle est jolie, Mlle Moïra" (*Moïra*, 124). Not long afterwards, Joseph moves to Mrs. Ferguson's house, and Moïra returns to her old room. On his first night in the new room, Joseph is struck with the conviction of his hopeless perdition. He is kept awake for the first time in his life by the irresistible attraction of a woman, whom he imagines sleeping in the very bed he had occupied the night before. He remembers the maid's comment, "Elle est jolie, Mlle Moïra."

Les images se reformaient d'elles-mêmes dans son cerveau par un mécanisme que rien ne pouvait fausser. . . . Quelque chose lui brûlait le sang. [*Moïra*, 151]

Near the end of the book, Joseph tells David that in his heart he had already committed the sin of fornication with Moïra the very first time he saw her.

The action of Joseph's story is an irresistible movement toward tragedy, and the atmosphere of fatality is too strong to be missed. This element of fatality, which I discussed earlier in connection with *Minuit*, is also one of the important similarities between *Moïra* and *Sud*. Green demonstrates in his *Journal* that he was conscious of the importance of fatality in writing *Moïra*. In a good example of the phenomenon of the *auto-critique*, he points out the irony of the fact that well-intentioned characters unwittingly provide Joseph with all the necessities for his crime. The preseminary student David, who otherwise has such a salutary effect on him, happens to show him one day the gardener's spade that Joseph later uses to bury his victim. He also gives Joseph a censored version of Shakespeare so that he can learn to understand "le coeur humain" without being shocked by the more licentious passages. Joseph is puzzled by the last scene of *Othello* and wonders why a man would kill the woman he loves. The manner in which Joseph kills Moïra—smothering her in his bed—recalls the end of *Othello*, and the blanket with which he smothers her was given to him by the Negro maid. The fact that other people unconsciously give Joseph the essentials of his crime is explained by Green in this way:

Ce sera une manière d'indiquer qu'il est à peu près irresponsable, qu'une sorte de fatalité le pousse dont Dieu tiendra compte. [J, 797]

This passage suggests that although the importance of fatality makes *Moïra* essentially a tragedy, it may be regarded as a Christian tragedy. In addition to the element of tragic destiny, there is evidence that points to the action of grace in the novel. The character of David is the most obvious example. Whenever Joseph is at the brink of desperation in his struggle, David offers him the consolation of a friend who shares many of his spiritual aspirations. David's room offers the security and serenity of the spiritual life that Joseph strives for. In one scene in particular, the two friends share a prayer in the darkness, and Joseph asks David whether one can be saved without having the certainty of salvation. David assures him: "Tu crois. Tu es sauvé" (*Moïra*, 113). And Joseph feels a unique moment of joy in that assurance.

Paradoxically, the character of Moïra, the mulatto temptress who is the instrument and symbol of Joseph's tragic fate, may also be interpreted from the perspective of grace. In the foreword that explains the significance of the name Moïra, Green also notes that it is of Celtic origin and is a modern variation in Ireland for Mary, as are the similar Irish forms Maura and Maureen. Moïra, then, is at least partly symbolic of the universally favorable aspect of woman in the sense that the Virgin Mary symbolizes compassion, mercy, and grace. Despite her obvious immorality, Moïra also has a beneficial effect on Joseph.

Before Joseph experiences the inevitable suffering of love (because of Moïra and Praileau), his inhumanity prevents him from acting charitably toward others. Praileau and Moïra lead Joseph through a stage of suffering in love that amounts to a passion, in the sense of Christ's passion.[4] It is a cathartic experience of what the human heart discovers in tragic love, and it ultimately teaches Joseph a new humility and understanding. Thus, Moïra's role in the action of divine grace is reminiscent of the connotations that arise from the name of Mauriac's heroine (Maria Cross) in *Le Désert de l'amour*.

Before Joseph Day gives in to his desires, his austere morality is a vestige of archaic puritanism. David tells him that although the world is impure, God has put us here to live and we must resign ourselves to the frailties of the human condition. Joseph's reply is characteristically violent.

> Prendre son parti de l'impureté du monde, c'est renier l'Evangile. . . . Je hais le monde. . . . Le monde est réprouvé. [*Moïra*, 95]

David explains that the sexual instinct is almost irresistible, and natural, at their age. "Je hais l'instinct sexuel," replies Joseph (*Moïra*, 110). Green's *Journal* calls *Moïra* "un long cri de colère contre l'instinct" (J, 795). In this sense the novel is indeed the tragic disillusionment of a young man who aspires to a form of sainthood that excludes the existence of sexuality.

In the conclusion of the novel, Moïra locks herself in the room with Joseph and waits for his self-control to break down. Both try to affect indifference: Moïra writes a letter to a friend while Joseph reads, ironically, *Othello*. In her letter, Moïra reveals that although she came to seduce Joseph, she now finds herself the seduced, thus further modifying her role of temptress. Finally, they violently consummate their passion, and Joseph then smothers Moïra in a fit of rage against the instrument of the loss of his chastity and his spiritual aspirations.

One of Joseph's last outcries against the sexuality that haunts him reveals the radical *dédoublement* that characterizes the Greenian protagonist who is beset with both spiritual and sensual obsessions.

Je désire horriblement ce péché que je ne commets pas. . . . J'ai quelquefois l'impression d'être séparé d'avec ma chair, et c'est comme s'il y avait en moi deux personnes dont l'une souffrirait et l'autre regarderait souffrir. [*Moïra*, 191]

The fundamental Greenian conflict of the two selves—the mystic who is radically separated from the flesh and the sensualist who is ensnared in the suffering of desire—is the tragic agon that Joseph Day illustrates so eloquently. It is a struggle whose resolution can be achieved only with the advent of the third self, the artist who expresses what he sees in the autonomous visionary realm that is the source of his fiction.

Julien Green's own experiences in the South were a fruitful point of departure for *Moïra*, which is among other things a beautiful recreation of Southern university life in the first quarter of this century. But the really evocative South, for Green, the cherished imaginary *pays lointain*, was the antebellum culture that Mary Hartridge Green had so nostalgically depicted to her children before she died. A novelist who is often preoccupied with the theme of escape has a natural affinity for exoticism, and in Green's works there is no more successful example of exoticism, both spatially and temporally, than the play *Sud*.

The elements of tragedy that were evident in *Moïra* are more fully developed in *Sud*. First staged at the Théâtre de l'Athénée-Louis Jouvet on March 6, 1953, Green's first play conformed admirably to the exigencies of classical tragedy, and the author offered a famous quotation of Aristotle as an apt summary of the action: "la purification d'une passion dangereuse par une libération véhémente." The play respects the unities of place and time. It begins on Sunday afternoon, April 11, 1861, the eve of the American Civil War, and ends at dawn the next day. The action takes place entirely at Bonaventure, the plantation of Edward Broderick, near Charleston, South Carolina, and each scene is set in the living room of the house. Even the *convenances* that were the rule in the seventeenth century are respected. All the violent action of the play occurs offstage and is described after the fact.

As for unity of action, Green himself offers an extremely incisive résumé of his play in the foreword. On the eve of the War Between the States, Lieutenant Ian Wiczewski encounters "la révélation de sa nature profonde et de l'amour le plus impérieux" immediately upon seeing Erik MacClure, whom he knew previously only by name. In desperation, he tries to avoid his fate by proposing to Angelina, whom MacClure had intended to marry. It is obvious that Ian does not love Angelina, and three other characters say so. Finally, after trying unsuccessfully to declare his passion to MacClure, Ian challenges him to a duel and intentionally dies at his hands (*Sud*, Avant-Propos).

The principal action of *Sud* is, like that of *L'Autre sommeil*, the discovery of the hero's homosexual nature. Unlike *L'Autre sommeil*, however, *Sud* takes place in a historical place and time that make the open avowal of homosexuality absolutely impossible. The result is an increased intensity of the inevitable tragic ending.

Although the play does conform to unity of action, there are three levels on which the action develops simultaneously. Green states in the Avant-Propos that he wrote *Sud* in reaction to the tradition that recently had degraded what he considered a "grave and noble subject" by confining it to the carnal level. The great actor Jean-Louis Barrault's first reaction to the play was that it would be difficult to act because of its multiple levels of meaning. For the discovery of Ian's erotic nature is not the only important aspect of the action of *Sud*.

The most obvious level of the action is of a political or social nature because of the historical context. The lengthy first act is mostly concerned with the political and social problems of the time, especially slavery. This act seems to indicate that the play will be focused thematically upon the issues that were dividing North and South in 1861.

Among the characters, Ian Wiczewski and Regina are the only non-Southerners. Regina is a cousin to the Brodericks and lives with them because of financial problems in her own family. She is staunchly opposed to slavery and cannot feel at home in the South. Wiczewski never pronounces on political issues and declares that his vocation as soldier requires him not to debate issues but to settle them in battle. Mrs. Strong is the *porte-parole* of the ideas of the Old South, and her argument with Regina heightens the importance of political issues.

The slavery question, which naturally arises in political contexts, is significant to all levels of interpretation in *Sud*. The theme of punishment especially relates slavery to the erotic and the spiritual dimensions of the play. In Act I, Broderick tells Regina that although she may hear Northerners disparage Southern plantation owners, she must realize that they have a mistaken impression of the situation. He continues:

As-tu jamais vu frapper un esclave à Bonaventure? . . . Je ne parle pas du fouet dont la seule idée fait horreur. [*Sud*, II, ii]

Later in the conversation, Mrs. Strong's arguments in favor of slavery offend Regina. When Regina asks to be excused from the room, Mrs. Strong says that in her day such an impertinent girl would have been flogged. Ian voices approval of the old methods.

Near the end of the first act, Broderick learns that his son Jimmy has slapped a disobedient slave. Broderick is outraged and asks Wiczewski to take Jimmy to the silo and use the old methods of discipline that he has approved. In lecturing his son, Broderick says Jimmy's treatment of the slave indicates the pride (*l'orgueil*) of his mother that survives in him. He wants the physical punishment to break Jimmy's pride. Regina pleads desperately with Broderick not to let Ian punish Jimmy. Later she confesses her reason to Angelina.

Il me semble que les coups qu'on donne à Jimmy c'est moi qui les reçois dans ma chair. La brutalité de cet homme est horrible! . . . Tu ne vois donc pas que c'est un bourreau? . . . J'aime le lieutenant Wiczewski à ne plus savoir que faire. . . . Il attend que ma bouche lui fasse l'aveu qui me transformerait en esclave. [*Sud*, I, v]

Jimmy unjustly punishes a slave and is punished in turn by Ian. In the confused Greenian erotic strategy of sadomasochism, Regina imagines herself as the punished. Ian has been making her suffer throughout the first act. Here she admits her neurotic passion and betrays her subconscious need for punishment at the hands of Ian. Ian is gratified sadistically, Regina, masochistically. It is an eroticism of slavery in which the humbling of one's pride is an essential aspect. Slavery, both as a social institution and as an erotic obsession, is based, then, on gratification of pride on one hand and submission on the other. Regina ends her confession to Angelina by making the same analogy between the two kinds of slavery.

Cet orgueil qui sera votre [the South's] ruine, je le sens dans le moindre geste que fait cet homme que j'adore. [*Sud*, I, v]

By the same token, when Ian suffers in his impossible passion for Erik MacClure, he speaks to him of pride.

Votre orgueil n'a jamais plié. Vous ne savez pas, comme je le sais maintenant, ce que c'est que l'asservissement d'une âme à une autre, ni le pouvoir de vie et de mort dont dispose un visage humain. [*Sud*, III, i][5]

For Regina, Lieutenant Wiczewski is *le bourreau*. In the opening scene he appears holding a riding crop that he carries with him most of the time. It is specifically mentioned in several instances. His vocation of soldier further involves him in violent conflict. And he is, of course, the one who administers Jimmy's punishment. Uncle John, an old blind freed slave who lives at Bonaventure, informs Broderick of his prophetic visions of divine punishment that will be accomplished in Broderick's house. He warns him that he has heard Ian's voice and that it is a cruel voice.

Ian's role in *Sud*, however, is just as ambivalent as Moïra's in Green's 1950 novel. At the end of Act I, Erik MacClure enters the living room of Bonaventure plantation. For Ian, it is a supremely fateful moment. The revelation of his impossible passion is immediate, devastating. Somewhat later, he describes the scene to Broderick, without, however, making an overt confession of his love. When he first saw MacClure, he also thought he saw another man standing next to him:

un homme vêtu comme un soldat, vêtu comme moi, mais le visage couvert d'un drap noir ou de quelque chose qui ressemblait à un vêtement qu'on lui aurait jeté sur la tête. [*Sud*, II, iv]

Ian has met his own *bourreau*, for MacClure's naïve insensitivity to Ian's attempts at confessing his passion cause Wiczewski to suffer violently. Like Regina, Ian loves the one who makes him suffer, and his erotic suffering humbles him in such a way that love is again a kind of slavery. What we learn of his childhood gives a clue to his predisposition to this sadomasochistic form of eroticism. He is an immigrant, having fled his native Poland during the insurrection of 1848. The Prussians had hanged his father for conspiracy. After the execution they had whipped young Ian as an example. Regina's reaction to this is predictably vengeful: "Cela m'est agréable de savoir qu'on vous a fouetté" (*Sud*, I, i).

The phenomenon of atavism seems to have held a peculiar interest for Green (there are numerous references to it in the *Journal*), and it is illustrated in a story, supposedly based on fact, that Ian tells Jimmy about a distant ancestor also named Ian, whose passion was an impossible one and eventually led to his death. The similarity between the stories of the two Ians is just one indication of the immense importance of destiny in *Sud*. The reminders of ineluctable, oppressive fate are ubiquitous in the play. There is first the constant menace of the war that everyone fears. The atmosphere itself is heavy, stifling. At the end of the second scene, Mrs. Strong says: "J'ai chaud. Je sens que cette fin de journée va être difficile. . . . Il n'y a pas d'air ici" (*Sud*, I, ii). Only a few lines later, Broderick declares, "Je ne puis rester dans cette pièce où j'étouffe" (*Sud*, I, iii). Ian finds it impossible to confess his love to Erik because of his situation of place and time. "L'air même que je respire ici est pour moi comme un bâillon" (*Sud*, III, i). Everything around him requires silence of him.

The old blind prophet Uncle John comes to warn his former master of his presentiments of impending disaster. He tells Broderick that he fears for Bonaventure because the wrath of God is going to be visited upon his house. Broderick later admits, "Ce qui se prépare est effrayant, j'en ai la certitude" (*Sud*, II, i). Ian himself realizes that, as Broderick has said, one cannot escape one's destiny, and he decides to hurl himself against his fate, as one would throw oneself against a wall. After the duel Erik MacClure concludes,

Il a fait de moi l'instrument d'une volonté plus forte que la nôtre. Nous ne pouvons rien à ce qui est prédestiné. [*Sud*, III, ii]

The dramatic moment when Ian sees the imaginary man standing behind MacClure is a unique example of the *dédoublement* phenomenon that is so common in Green's fiction. It is the kind of fictional moment that involves the visionary third self of the artist in a profound sense. We have already suggested that the imaginary person Ian sees is his *bourreau* because he is dressed in black and hooded. The vision warns him that MacClure will be the one who makes him suffer. But the imaginary person is also said to be dressed like a soldier, like Ian, and in the final scene of the play, Ian's body is brought on stage with his black tunic over his head to cover the ugly wounds of the duel. Thus, Ian's vision is not only of his *bourreau*, but also of himself and the fate to which he is finally to succumb.

A significant if implicit comment on Ian's predisposition to inversion is the fact that his duel with MacClure takes place near the silo, the same place where he punished young Jimmy. The duel completes a series of fights that Green describes in erotic terms: the struggle with the *aspirant* in *Mille chemins ouverts* (pp. 212-13) and Joseph's fight with Praileau in *Moïra* (pp. 28-31). The duel, along with the punishment of Jimmy, is an illustration of the erotic slavery that controls Ian's emotional life. One of the witnesses of the duel describes it in this manner:

> Le lieutenant ne s'est pas défendu. Au début, si, un peu, mais à la fin son visage a changé d'aspect. On le sentait offert comme une victime à cette fureur qu'il avait déchaînée. [*Sud*, III, ii]

The primary action of *Sud* is the erotic story of Ian Wiczewski. It follows relentlessly the pattern of tragedy, with foreshadowings of Ian's tragic destiny in an oppressive atmosphere of impending disaster that is intensified by the threat of war. But the historical and erotic elements are not the only significant aspects of the play. There is also the spiritual dimension, which has a definite effect on both the erotic and the historical interpretations.

The two most profoundly spiritual characters of *Sud* are Regina and Uncle John. The latter is a true visionary, a devout man who hears the voice of the Lord and relates its message to the people with whom he lives. He senses God's disapproval of slavery and the divine justice that will necessarily ensue. Perhaps more significantly, he warns Broderick of Ian's cruelty. Uncle John is blind, but he has a special kind of clairvoyance. He does not see the things of this world but is intimately attuned to the things of the spirit. His role is reminiscent of Iaokanann's in Flaubert's *Hérodias*. Iaokanann and Uncle John are representatives of an oppressed people who prophesy to the figures of power in their respective eras the wrath of God that is to be visited on them. Each speaks in the tradition of Elijah and the other Hebrew prophets.

The menace of war takes its greatest toll on Broderick, the owner of the Bonaventure plantation. Under the stress of events he says: "Je voudrais avoir la foi de Regina. . . . Elle croit, elle s'appuie sur quelqu'un ou quelque chose qu'on ne voit pas" (*Sud*, I, iii). Regina's faith, although rather unorthodox, is indeed strong. She does not believe in the Trinity, the divinity of Jesus, or baptism. "Je crois simplement en Dieu, le Dieu du Christ qui est en nous tous" (*Sud*, I, v).

At the beginning of *Sud*, Ian Wiczewski, like Joseph Day, has never been in love. His lack of experience in love, again like Joseph's, leads him to cause others to suffer. Once Ian experiences suffering in his own passion for MacClure, he understands what he has done to Regina and asks her forgiveness. Knowing that his death is at hand, he tells her that he does not want to leave her without asking for her pardon. "Depuis quelques heures, j'ai compris. Je souffre comme vous et de la même manière peut-être. Il y a ce lien entre nous" (*Sud*, III, i). Regina does not answer Ian's request for forgiveness until the final scene of the play, in which she is the incarnation of the feminine role of mercy and grace that Moïra only dimly suggests. Alone with Ian's hooded corpse, she addresses him softly, "comme la mère parle à l'enfant qui dort" (*Sud*, III, ii). She tells him that although she had remained silent when he asked for pardon, her heart was bursting. "Dieu essuiera toutes les larmes. Il l'a dit lui-même. Il essuiera tes larmes et les miennes" (*Sud*, III, ii).

Green states in the foreword to *Sud* that Ian's sin is not his love for Erik MacClure, even though that would have been the verdict of his society. His sin, says Green, is having made Regina suffer so cruelly. The hamartia that leads to the downfall of this tragic protagonist is the sadomasochism of his psychological nature that makes love a form of slavery for him. The "dangerous passion" that Aristotle says must be purified through the cathartic experience of tragedy is not, then, Ian's passion for MacClure, but the obsession with pride and submission that characterizes the violent forms of love in *Sud*.

Moïra and *Sud* together give a powerful impression of the world of violence that is the South for Julien Green. It is an imaginary setting for some of the most devastating clashes between erotic and spiritual forces in his fictional realm. Both mystical and erotic forces are expressed in terms of violence: the whip, fire, punishment, slavery, war, duels, and crimes. These two works are intensely tragic both in their sustained atmosphere and in their conclusions. But tragic fate in each is accompanied by indications of the action of grace. This paradoxical combination of tragic fatality and grace in *Moïra* and *Sud* is indicative of a general trend that characterizes all of Green's writing since 1950, a trend that I shall discuss in the next chapter.

Chapter Six

The Concept of the Third Self

If Julien Green is not simply a mystic, if he is not most profoundly a sensualist, then his most nearly integral identity lies in a third self. The image of the mystic was made abundantly clear in his *Journal* and the sensualist found its most complete revelation in the autobiography. I have given close attention to some of Green's fictional works with the intention of providing documentation for an interpretation of the third Greenian self, the one which owes its very existence to the fictional reality.

In the *Journal*, Green states repeatedly that his novels constitute his true diary. Modern criticism has increasingly subscribed to Mallarmé's contention that the artist's true identity may be appreciated only from his imaginative creations: "Tel qu'en Lui-même enfin l'éternité le change" (*Le Tombeau d'Edgar Poe*). Proust's *Contre Sainte-Beuve* (published in 1954) strengthened the position of the Bergsonian *moi profond* by leveling a stinging indictment of the critical tendency to rely too heavily on an artist's biography. Indeed, the subject of much of the art and literature of the last hundred years has been the incarnation of the artist himself. The Socratic quest that was instrumental in both Green's *Journal* and his autobiography is equally important in his fiction, where the self is liberated and passes through new transformations that lead to a personal myth of the artist.

Julien Green was destined to arrive at his own myth of the artist because of his method of writing. As I mentioned in Chapter Three, he has never believed in making a preliminary outline of a book because he never knows in advance what will happen in it. He writes only what he sees his characters in the process of acting out. Therefore, he does not invent; he recounts what he witnesses. For this reason, writing fiction is for Green as much a process of discovery as of creation. His characters lead him to a fuller understanding of his true self. The fictional self, then, has a spark of authenticity that is not equalled in the confessional context because of its spontaneous origins.

Il y a, pour un romancier, une réalité conventionnelle et une réalité qu'on pourrait appeler une réalité de vision. . . . La vérité de vision demande un effort beaucoup plus rude, une espèce de don de soi. [J, 51]

It is not enough to describe a character's actions. The Greenian novelist must see *par le dedans* what the words describe.

Green's fictional reality imposes itself on him in the form of an intense vision in which he must participate.

Le vrai romancier ne domine pas son roman, il devient son roman, il s'y plonge. Entre lui et ses personnages, la complicité est plus profonde même qu'il ne le croit et s'ils pèchent, il pèche aussi de quelque manière. Il est tout ce qu'est son livre, s'il y croit, s'il se laisse prendre; et s'il ne se laisse pas prendre, s'il ne subit pas lui-même l'envoûtement de cette chose monstrueuse qui sort de son cerveau—car le roman est un monstre—il n'écrit plus de romans, il en fabrique. [J, 588]

According to Green, the novelist must become what he is writing. Indeed, he himself had no alternative. Perhaps the strongest motive in all of Green's writing is to find a kind of rebirth, "changer, devenir autre, souci constant" (J, 361). The desire to become *autre* partly explains the attraction that metempsychosis had for him. The hero of *Si j'étais vous*, Fabien Especel, has the power to be reincarnated as different persons, and other Greenian protagonists project certain aspects of their own personalities as doubles. The tranformations that fiction provided Green were the only means by which he was able to discover a self that he could live with.

Writing fiction is a compulsive activity for most serious novelists, but the case of Julien Green is an extreme one. He says in the diary that without that vocation, he might well have gone insane. "Je trompe la violence qui forme le fond de ma nature en écrivant mes livres. . . . On se délivre de beaucoup de rêves en écrivant" (J, 9, 930). Because of the turmoil that has always raged within him, because of a life-style of self-imposed solitude, Green has always been obliged to write his novels in order to maintain his psychological equilibrium. It is the most efficacious means at his disposal for exorcising the demons of his divided self.

Green's method of writing has had great therapeutic value for him, but by the same token it has intensified a dramatic debate within him which he has discussed in the *Journal*. Is the act of writing a novel compatible with the state of grace? Can the artist live otherwise than in sin? The answer: "Tirez l'écrivain de son péché et il n'écrit plus" (J, 950). The very source of fiction, according to Green, is essentially involved in the realm of the impure, and if the artist tries to purify the source there is no more fiction.

Thus, the vocations of novelist and of Christian appear incompatible, and the problem of art and morality is a very disturbing one for Green. His close friend Jacques Maritain, who had an important influence on his spiritual development, wrote about the problem of the two vocations in a very Greenian vein in *Art et Scolastique*. He agreed that art is pagan in origin and inevitably involved in sin. Even though it is very difficult, it is not impossible to combine the two vocations of novelist and Christian. The essential difficulty is that "il s'agit de mettre en paix deux absolus."[1]

For art is, according to Maritain, an absolute. It is a fully autonomous domain that can never be subjected to morality. Its sole end is the creation of beauty, whereas the end of morality is reconciliation with God. Maritain goes to great lengths to establish the unquestionable purity of art. "L'Artiste est soumis, dans la ligne de son art, à une sorte d'ascétisme, qui peut exiger des sacrifices héroïques."[2]

In the character of Daniel O'Donovan, Julien Green discovered intuitively this heroic destiny. The vocation of artist called for him to descend into the abyss of the unknown within him, a perilous unknown peopled with erotic and spiritual obsessions. The heroic role of the visionary artist developed in Green's mind to the point of representing a personal myth in his later fiction. In *L'Autre sommeil*, he became increasingly aware of the gift of seeing by means of *la seconde vue* of the visionary artist. In *Le Visionnaire*, the figure of Manuel recounting his vision was one version of the third self incarnated.

Le Voyageur sur la terre and *L'Autre sommeil*, however, were not typical of Green's early fiction because of their highly autobiographical content. Most of what he wrote before 1950 was apparently very unlike him. His own *vérité* was clothed in mystery in these early works, which were full of female protagonists and fantastic plots that bore little resemblance to his own life. Even his unobtrusive style was designed to hide the personality of the author. Because of his fictional disguise Julien Green was not recognized in his early works. *L'Autre sommeil*, for example, was never really understood as a kind of confession until the last part of Green's career. The theme of sexual inversion in it was long ignored, as it was in *Moïra* and even *Sud*. Indeed, the drama of Ian Wiczewski and Erik MacClure was initially taken to be a historical play about the problems of the South in 1861. Not until the great confession of *Partir avant le jour* did the public appreciate the true importance of the erotic in Green's works.

The evolution of Green criticism has followed a pattern quite similar to that of Green's fiction itself. Before 1939, his novels were involved in a seemingly unautobiographical world of hallucination and were interpreted as examples of a *réalisme magique*. In the 1940s, his novels were less popular and the importance of religion in his diary led critics to regard him as essentially a Catholic writer. With the increasingly autobiographical accent of *Moïra*, the trilogy of plays,[3] *Chaque homme dans sa nuit*, and, of course, the autobiography itself, critics began slowly to accept the erotic aspect of Green's fiction and to appreciate the violence of the conflict in which it was born. Green himself became more aware of having found a vocation in expressing his deepest *vérité*.

> Jamais un scrupuleux ne fera un grand roman. Dans la crainte d'offenser Dieu, il écrira de prudentes platitudes, et qui sait si Dieu ne veut pas le risque? Qui sait si ce n'est pas là le moyen de lui plaire et d'accomplir sa vocation? [J, 588]

The image that recurs most frequently in Green's works is the staircase, which I have noted at moments of dramatic intensity in the course of this study. The author himself was the first to discover the obsessive recurrence of the staircase in his writing. In the April 4, 1933, entry of his diary he listed examples of stairways in moments of fear or other intense emotions in nearly all the novels and short stories he had written at that point in his career. Since that time, there have been numerous interpretations of the staircase image ranging from the obvious Freudian connotations to the equally obvious notion of the mystic's progess toward heaven.

In *Le Voyageur sur la terre*, the old captain's nightly climbing of the stairs throws Daniel O'Donovan into fits of superstitious fear. Denis in *L'Autre sommeil* is seated on a stairway when his erotic fantasy ends in a swoon. Once in *Minuit* and twice in *Moïra* the creaking of the stair as the protagonist mounts toward his room reminds him of the crack of a whip. Green tells us in *Terre lointaine* that as a boy he often wrote stories in which he was being chased on a staircase and had to take refuge in a basement. In these stories he imagined himself killing many people.

In *Memories of Happy Days* he recounts the nightly drama of having to go to bed before the older members of the family during the summers at Andrésy. Much too frightened to go all the way upstairs to his dark room, he would sit on the stairway and read. The painful ordeal of the *drame du coucher* was a poignantly oedipal one in the same sense that it was for Marcel as he reluctantly climbed the familiar stairway in Proust's *Du Côté de chez Swann*. It was this experience, suggests Green, that was the origin of the prominence of the staircase image in his fiction.

There was, however, another important experience in Green's life that helped crystallize the staircase image in his mind. The moment that determined his fate, he says in the diary, came one afternoon in April of 1919 as he was leaving the crypt of the chapel at the Rue Cortambert.

> En remontant l'escalier de la crypte, je me suis arrêté un instant sur une marche, le coeur débordant de tristesse à l'idée du monde que j'allais quitter, ainsi que tout ce qu'il aurait pu me donner et que je refusais pour me retirer dans un monastère. . . . Tout à coup je sentis se formuler en moi "le grand refus" qui devait prêter à ma vie un aspect si particulier. [J, 385]

Indeed, the great refusal of monasticism was a fateful decision in his life, and it was to result in the nostalgia for sainthood that never could be satisfied. In that moment, it seemed that all the world was being offered him: "Sortant d'une espèce de Moyen Age, j'abordais en pleine Renaissance" (J, 385). After leaving the chapel, he was sure that his life had just reached an important turning point. He was moving away from the realm of the spirit and beginning to explore the strange world of the flesh that was beckoning to him.

I have already mentioned the analogies between the sensualist and the mystic. According to Green, their common ground is that each is in search of the absolute. The seemingly conflicting forces of eroticism and mysticism in Green's works are ultimately directed toward the same goal and must be understood as such. For this reason, the staircase image is significant as a *liaison* between the first two selves of Julien Green, and points toward the visionary third self.

To reduce literature to a purely erotic interpretation is to rob it of its true richness of meaning. As Mircéa Eliade has observed, Freud's weakness in this matter was that he never understood that sexuality is not pure, that it is a phenomenon with richly varied aspects and one whose supreme function, perhaps, is cosmological. "Sauf pour le monde moderne, la sexualité a été partout et toujours une hiérophanie et l'acte sexuel un acte intégrale (donc, *aussi* un moyen de connaissance)."[4] In discussing the symbolism of the center, Eliade cites Green's use of the staircase as an example of an *axis mundi*.

L'escalade ou l'ascension symbolise *le chemin vers la réalité absolue*; et, dans la conscience profane, l'approche de cette réalité provoque un sentiment ambivalent de peur et de joie, d'attraction et de répulsion, etc. Les idées de sanctification, de mort, d'amour et de délivrance sont impliquées dans le symbolisme de l'escalier. En effet, chacun de ces modes d'être représente l'abolition de la condition humaine profane, c'est-à-dire une rupture de nouveau ontologique.[5]

Julien Green's fiction is the meeting place of various levels of being. The third self is the consciousness that recounts in a visionary manner the communication between cosmic zones for the reader. The staircase illustrates the phenomenon of analogous realities in Green's fiction. Another image that is closely related to this visionary quality is that of the threshold. In *Mille chemins ouverts* we saw the adolescent Green immobile on the threshold of a friend's room as he contemplated his captivating beauty. In *Le Voyageur sur la terre* I called Daniel's decision to leave home a threshold experience. When Ian first sees his *bourreau* in *Sud*, Erik is standing immobile in the threshold of the plantation house (I, v). Similarly, Denis of *L'Autre sommeil* says that the nude statues he contemplates in hallucinatory fashion exist on the threshold of an unexplored world (AS, 118), and in the diary, Green tells us that *Le Visionnaire*, a book that obviously explores communication between levels of reality, was originally to be entitled *Au Seuil de la nuit* (J, 129-30). In *Partir avant le jour*, Green speaks of the ineffable secrets of God that only children hear and that are forgotten as we leave the world of childhood. He says that in seeking to regain the intuitive revelations of childhood, he knows that he must remain silent because they are hidden beneath the threshold of language (PAJ, 46).

The images of the staircase and the threshold reveal the ultimate drama of Green's fiction. They occur at moments when the protagonist is on the verge of discovering a new reality. Often it is the shattering revelation of sexuality, the impure realm that is so fearful to the product of puritanical heritage. Sometimes it is a fleeting glimpse of the mystical reality to which the first Greenian self aspires.

Janine Carrel defines the threshold experience as one which "après avoir révélé l'existence d'un univers divin dissimulé en-deçà du monde et de la vie terrestre, ramène l'homme dans un monde terrestre où il peut trouver l'accomplissement de son destin dans un présent qui participe de l'éternité divine et où Dieu s'incarne."[6] The threshold experience is much more than an intermediate position between divine and earthly realities. It is a moment of passage in which self-annihilation and rebirth are involved in the hero's progress toward the universal source.[7] It partakes of the artist's mythic role of visionary hero. As with Daniel O'Donovan, Julien Green's vocation entails a perilous interior descent through the metamorphoses of the self that culminates in "the source of living waters."

The puritanical heritage of Julien Green made it impossible for his first self, the mystic, to transcend his second identity, the sensualist. The horror of sexual inversion for the Puritan mystic rendered him incapable of resolving his identity crisis in religious terms. The third self of the visionary artist was the only identity that Green could assume in order to integrate the various aspects of his own personality. In his most recent works we find the basic duality of spirit and eros in its most finished form. The current stage of his fiction began in 1950 with *Moïra*. His three plays, especially *L'Ennemi*, explored the struggle in increasing depth. *Chaque homme dans sa nuit* represents an even more radical polarization of forces in the character of Wilfred Ingram, the *coureur* who is also the chosen vessel of divine grace. Finally, in *L'Autre* the polarity is expressed in still another *dédoublement*. There are two main characters, each of whom has his own narrative, as in *Le Visionnaire*. And, as in *L'Ennemi*, there is a dual movement of spiritual and erotic forces represented by the two main characters. Significantly, a great deal of this long novel is devoted not to narrative but to dialogue between Karin and Roger, constant debates between spirit and flesh.

The evolution in Green's career that I have just outlined gains added dimensions in the light of one of Jacques Petit's most significant theories. According to Petit, one of the most essential sources of Green's writings was an experience that is described in *Terre lointaine*. Mark, the student at the University of Virginia whom Green had loved silently for two years, was visiting his friend in Paris in 1923. As they strolled together by the Seine, Green resolved at last to tell Mark of his passion but was unable to confess the nature of his feelings. Petit observes that there are repeated variations of this scene of "l'aveu impossible" throughout Green's novels up until 1960. Denis and Claude in *L'Autre sommeil*, Simon and Joseph in *Moïra*, and Ian and Erik in *Sud* are examples of the male's impossible avowal of homosexual passion, and the examples of heterosexual and/or female versions of the scene are numerous.

In *Chaque homme dans sa nuit* (1960), however, Angus actually does confess his love for Wilfred by means of a letter. This scene, says Petit, marks the resolution of an all-important theme in Green's fiction which he calls "le poids d'un silence."[8] Significantly, *Chaque homme dans sa nuit* was the last book written by Green before his autobiography, which is a uniquely frank and explicit confession of his personal erotic drama that had been only partly revealed by any of his preceding works.

The movement of self-discovery and of confession throughout Green's career may thus be understood as culminating in his autobiography. In the early stages of his writing, he was unable to face his most disquieting problems and deal with them directly. The motive of escape, then, is naturally the most prevalent one in the early fiction. With *Moïra*, Green seemed to have found a new determination to explore more thoroughly the meaning of his own erotic drama. The increasingly autobiographical aspect of the fiction beginning with *Moïra* is a reflection of this determination. Indeed, the end of *Moïra* suggests a turning point not only in Joseph Day's life but also in the life of his spiritual cousin Julien Green.

After Joseph has submitted to the loss of his virginity and committed the murder, Bruce Praileau offers him a means of escape. The fact that Joseph accepts Praileau's proposal and begins his flight is characteristic of the abortive escapes in the conclusions of Green's earlier novels. While he is fleeing through the woods, he takes satisfaction in the deepening snow that has fallen since he buried Moïra, knowing it will abet his escape attempt. Joseph, at this point, is fleeing from the dreaded sexual instinct that Moïra represents and vainly seeking to recapture the inhuman purity (represented by the snow[9]) that characterized him before he met Moïra. But the cathartic experience of tragic suffering he has undergone is effectual. Finally, he decides to return, to give himself up, to face his realities, and to confess his crime.

In writing *Moïra*, Green was embarking on a new stage of writing characterized by more direct self-discovery and confession. The tragic conclusions of *Moïra, Sud, L'Ennemi, Chaque homme dans sa nuit*, and *L'Autre* all suggest the possibility, at the same time, of the action of grace. The avowal of homosexual passion was impossible for Green's heroes until the definitive confession of the autobiography. The resulting "poids d'un silence" was important in lending a special tension and mystery to the pre-autobiography novels. Now that Green has finally exorcised the demons of his divided self in the autobiography, the question is whether those demons, whether that weight of silence, were essential to the fertility of his artistic creation.

L'Autre (1971) has, indeed, much less of the authenticity of the Greenian fiction of the 1950s. It is somewhat longer and tends to belabor the duality of spirit and flesh, which all somehow seems to have been said before. The duality in *L'Autre* is too neatly delineated in a rather self-conscious fashion. Likewise, the fourth volume of the autobiography (*Jeunesse*, 1974) is still more explicit than the previous and none the better for it. *Jeunesse*, when compared to *Terre lointaine*, lacks much of the tension of the shadowy erotic identity struggling to express itself.

Obviously, it is too soon to know, but one is led to ask whether Green's autobiography has drained the mystery from the richest source of his inspiration. It appears that any future works inevitably will be either less ingenuous than *Moïra* and *Chaque homme dans sa nuit* or will mark a radically new stage in his writing. Will Green's long career—*né avec le siècle*—once again renew itself in a different vein, as Hugo's so often did in spanning the century before Green?

It was a mysterious process by which the myth of the visionary artist imposed itself on Julien Green. While it was still an unconscious myth it expressed itself in starkly primitive form. When he was drawing pictures as a child, he felt the first effects of the mysterious identity within that insisted on expressing itself.

> Un mécanisme intellectuel accomplissait un redoutable progrès. L'hallucination se changeait en système. En vérité tout dessin devenait inutile parce qu'il se faisait dans mon esprit une représentation fascinante au sens le plus fort du terme. Ce que j'imaginais, je le voyais comme un visionnaire voit une vision. [PAJ, 310]

In this sense, the mysterious identity of *l'autre* in Green's most recent novel may be considered the third self of the artist. The evolution of Green's writing has been a movement from mystery to self-discovery, during which the transformations of the self have led him to the most profound revelation of his *vérité*. Although the mechanisms of the third self are obscure, its presence is unmistakable, as Green indicates in the following passage:

> A propos du roman que j'écris, je voudrais dire ceci, qui est vrai de tous mes livres: il arrive un moment où de grandes brêches se forment par où

passe quelque chose qui ne vient pas de moi, mais d'un autre dont parfois j'ai peur comme d'un moi plus impérieux, plus autoritaire et plus sûr de lui que le moi que je connais. Quel écrivain n'a éprouvé cela? Et d'où cela vient-il? [J, 1170]

In Green's introduction to an English translation of Péguy, he included parenthetically this amplification on the idea that Péguy's own poetry had a providential influence in leading him to his conversion. "What lies deepest in us is very often beyond our ken until we go through the struggle to express it, and then it begins to react on us."[10] Green's writing has led him to the revelation of a hidden identity, a self that witnesses with the eyes of *la seconde vue* a fictional reality with a unique visionary quality.

Notes

Introduction

1. Robert de Saint-Jean, *Julien Green par lui-même* (Paris, 1967), pp. 6-7.
2. "Un Américain à Paris," *Le Monde*, June 4, 1971, p. 18.
3. Baptized Julian Hartridge Green, he adopted the French equivalent of his given name when he began to publish.
4. Charles Baudelaire, *Oeuvres complètes* (Paris, 1961), p. 1277.
5. References to the *Journal* by the abbreviation "J" and page number come from the one-volume edition, *Journal (1928-1958)*. References by date come from the more recent edition, *Journal II (1949-1966)*. Facts of publication for all of Green's works cited here will be found in the bibliography at the back of this book.
6. Even though this statement comes from the period of his separation from the Church, his feelings on the matter have not changed.
7. Charles Moëller, *Littérature du XXe siècle et christianisme* (Paris and Tournai, 1953), pp. 302-70.
8. Even the first two personality analyses to appear in professional publications are quite unsatisfactory because of the lack of material available for documentation: Milton C. Albrecht, "A Study of Julian Green," *Journal of Abnormal and Social Psychology* 41 (April 1946): 169-88; idem, "Psychological Motives in the Fiction of Julian Green," *Journal of Personality* 16 (March 1948): 278-303. Albrecht concludes in the former that "the possibility of tendencies other than for heterosexual relationships must be discarded for lack of evidence; even the dreams printed in the journal show no such tendencies" (p. 181).
9. Dominique Fernandez, "Comment on devient homosexuel," *La Quinzaine littéraire* 2 (April 1, 1966): 6-7; and Marcel Eck, "La Genèse d'une angoisse: essai de psychanalyse de Julien Green," *La Table ronde* 196 (May 1964): 130-44.

Chapter One

1. Georges Poulet, *Etudes sur le temps humain*, vol. 4, *Mesure de l'instant* (Paris, 1968), p. 345.
2. There are significant similarities between the Flaubertian saints (Saint Julien and Saint Antoine) and the mystical self of Julien Green. It is little wonder that Flaubert has been one of his great personal favorites.
3. See Samuel Stokes, *Julian Green and the Thorn of Puritanism* (New York, 1955), pp. 53-79.

4. Marc Eigeldinger, it may be noted, alluded to Green's attitude toward reality in the title of his *Julien Green et la tentation de l'irréel* (Paris, 1947).

5. Stéphane Mallarmé, "Hamlet," *Crayonnés au théâtre* from *Oeuvres complètes* (Paris, 1945), p. 299.

6. This is Green's only book to have been written in English and his first attempt at autobiography. But it was written also as a tribute to France at one of her most trying historical moments, and for this reason the nostalgic evocation of happy times prevented the author from delving into the more disturbing experiences of his youth. The most valuable part of the book is the last chapters, which recount Green's debut in the world of letters, encounters with great writers, and some of the ideas and experiences that lay behind the composition of his first novels.

7. See Eck, "La genèse d'une angoisse," and Fernandez, "Comment on devient homosexuel."

8. Similarly, Joseph Day anxiously asks his friend David Laird whether it is possible to be saved without being absolutely sure of salvation. "Tu crois. Tu es sauvé," answers David (*Moïra*, 113).

9. The ubiquity of violent crime in Green's fiction is partly an exteriorization of the author's guilt feelings about his erotic life, his puritanical background having inculcated in him the equivalence of sex and sin. Crime in his adolescent hallucinations was a form of revolt against the claustration of rigid moral restraints imposed by the parents, real or imaginary.

10. See Michel Guiomar, "L'incendie de Mont-Cinère: préface à une topoanalyse de Julien Green," *La Revue d'esthétique* 20 (1967): 74-87, for a Bachelardian interpretation of the house in *Mont-Cinère* as main character.

11. Reproductions of this painting appear in Saint-Jean, *Julien Green par lui-même*, p. 17; and Jean Sémolué, *Julien Green: ou l'obsession du mal* (Paris, 1964), opposite p. 64.

12. Sémolué, *L'obsession du mal*, p. 34.

13. The image of the whip in young Julien's drawing of naked criminals (PAJ, 51) will recur in erotic situations in other works.

14. This scene is recast as fiction in the opening pages of *Chaque homme dans sa nuit*.

Chapter Two

1. For a discussion of the similarities and differences in the mystical doctrines of religious mythologies and those of psychoanalysis, see Joseph Campbell, *The Hero with a Thousand Faces* (New York, 1949), pp. 164-65.

2. Although written in 1925, prior to the composition of *Mont-Cinère*, it was not published until 1927, after *Mont-Cinère*.

3. Cf. the importance of the staircase image in other contexts. Green himself enumerates the salient examples of the motif from the novels in an entry of the *Journal*, p. 111.

4. *Webster's Seventh New Collegiate Dictionary*, 14th ed. (Springfield, Mass.: G & C. Merriam Co., 1961).

5. Cf. the "cercle magique" of solitude resulting from the adolescent Green's sexual innocence, as discussed in Chapter One, above.

6. Dante often is encouraged by Virgil to be less dependent on his guidance, especially toward the end of the ascent of Mt. Purgatory, which is allegorically the purification of Dante's will.

7. The threshold experience is an extremely characteristic one in the Greenian drama, and I shall develop its significance in Chapter Six.

8. Evelyn Underhill, *Mysticism: A Study in the Nature and Development of Man's Spiritual Consciousness*, 11th ed. (London, 1926), p. 246.

9. When Virgil leaves Dante at the summit of the mount of purgation, he says:

> "Libero, dritto e sano è tuo arbitrio,
> E fallo fora non fare a suo senno;
> Per ch'io te sopra te corono e mitrio."
> [*Purgatorio* 27: 140-42]

10. The conversation is later revealed to be totally a product of Daniel's imagination.

11. The same biblical quotation on the façade of the University of Virginia was striking to the young Green, who was to learn his own *vérité* there.

12. Northrop Frye, *Anatomy of Criticism* (New York, 1967), p. 193.

13. Campbell, *Hero*, pp. 245-46; Frye, *Anatomy*, pp. 33, 36-37.

14. Moëller, *Littérature du XXe siècle et christianisme*, pp. 302-70.

15. Campbell, *Hero*, p. 173.

16. Frye, *Anatomy*, p. 193.

Chapter Three

1. The sensual curve of rounded limbs, it may be remembered, is an obsessive motif in Green's homosexual awakening as recounted in the autobiography.

2. Note the recurrence of the stairway image at a moment of dramatic intensity.

3. Jacques Petit, *Julien Green: "l'homme qui venait d'ailleurs,"* (Paris, 1969), p. 105.

4. Cf. Baudelaire's "Moesta et Errabunda," in which the poet speaks of "le vert paradis des amours enfantines."

5. Pascal, *Oeuvres Complètes* (Paris: Gallimard, 1954), p. 1205.

6. In a personal interview with M. Green in Paris in April of 1971, I made the analogy of the importance of the visual image in his works to the visionary aspect of his writing and asked him to describe for me the way in which the faculty of "la seconde vue," as Father Moëller calls it, operates in him. He agreed that in composing a novel or play he sees things as a painter would see them, but he went on to say that seeing the unfolding of a fictional work within him was also quite different from the normal faculty of vision. He spoke of moments when he lies recumbent in a very relaxed frame of mind, often just before he falls asleep or just as he is waking. At such moments "I do see something," he told me, "something inside me that corresponds to a sort of vision." Entire scenes emerge from his memory in the order of the subconscious, sometimes streets he has walked, sometimes churches he has visited, and very often people who have remained in his memory.

Chapter Four

1. See Chapter Three, note 6, above.

2. In Green's fiction, variations on the image of the whip recur in erotically intense situations that involve sadomasochism and/or homosexuality. Compare the importance of the whip image here to its development in the main character of *Sud*, Ian Wiczewski, as discussed in Chapter Five, below.

3. Marcel Proust, *A la recherche du temps perdu* 2 (Paris, 1954): 770.

4. In Greek, the Fates were called the Moirai, one of the origins of the title of Green's 1950 novel *Moïra*.

5. Cf. p. 40 of *Minuit*, where the floor squeaks with the sound of a whip. Note again the image of the whip, which evokes erotic suffering and sadomasochism, reminiscent of *Le Visionnaire* and anticipatory of *Moïra* and *Sud*.

Chapter Five

1. Saint-Jean, *Green par lui-même*, p. 95.

2. In a personal interview (Paris, April 1971), M. Green told me that the various urban scenes of this novel correspond to mental images of places he saw in New York, Baltimore, Philadelphia, and other American cities, in addition to the scenes that take place in the South, notably Wormsloe, whose counterpart in reality is an antebellum house located just outside Savannah.

3. In the *Inferno*, Canto I, Dante meets three beasts that impede his progress along the hill of virtue. The beasts are normally interpreted as representative of the three main categories of sin, and the most troublesome one for Dante is "una lupa" (1. 49), which symbolizes Incontinence. Although another of the animals, the lion, symbolizes Violence in the *Inferno*, Joseph Day's violent temperament may be understood as a form of incontinence, especially since Green often states that violent crimes—such as Joseph's—are the logical results of ravenous sensuality. Moïra represents the wild, bestial incontinence that is Joseph's undoing. Her obsessive influence on his sexual desires, which he struggles to suppress, is aptly described by Dante's she-wolf, which stalks him "senza pace" (1. 58).

4. Charles Moëller in *Littérature du XXe siècle et christianisme* uses Joseph Day's "passion" to illustrate Green's own cathartic experience of suffering in love, the "épreuve de la tentation" (p. 315) that was to give the writer's testimony a new resonance, once he finally returned to the Church.

5. Cf. the motif of slavery in Green's fantasies of masculine beauty during his university years (Chapter One, above).

Chapter Six

1. Jacques Maritain, *Art et Scolastique* (Paris, 1927), p. 112.

2. Ibid., p. 135.

3. The exteriorization of Green's erotic and spiritual drama on the stage in the 1950s must have had a therapeutic effect never before experienced by him with his novels. The plays are, in a sense, a prelude to the deep self-discovery of the 1960s.

4. Mircéa Eliade, *Images et symboles: essais sur le symbolisme magico-religieux* (Paris, 1952), p. 16.

5. Ibid., p. 51.

6. Janine Carrel, *L'Expérience du seuil dans l'oeuvre du Julien Green* (Zurich, 1967), p. 103.

7. Campbell, *Hero*, pp. 81-91.

8. Petit, *Julien Green*, pp. 24-31.

9. Curiously enough, despite his obsession with purity, Green almost never employs the image of snow. But the symbolic value of the image is inescapable in this context.

10. Introduction to Charles Péguy, *Basic Verities: Prose and Poetry* (New York, 1943), trans. by Ann and Julian Green, p. 26.

Selected Bibliography

WORKS BY JULIEN GREEN

"The Apprentice Psychiatrist." *University of Virginia Magazine* 63 (May-June 1920): 334-46.

[Théophile Delaporte (pseud.)]. "Pamphlet contre les catholiques de France." *La Revue des Pamphlétaires* 1 (October 15, 1924).

Mont-Cinère. Paris: Plon, 1926.

Adrienne Mesurat. Paris: Plon, 1927.

Léviathan. Paris: Plon, 1929.

Le Voyageur sur la terre [first published by Gallimard, 1927]; *Les Clefs de la mort; Christine; Léviathan*. Paris: Plon, 1930.

L'Autre sommeil. Geneva and Paris: Ed. de la Palatine, 1950 [first published by Gallimard, 1931].

Epaves. Paris: Plon, 1932.

Le Visionnaire. Paris: Plon, 1934.

Minuit. Paris: Plon, 1936.

Varouna. Paris: Plon, 1940.

Memories of Happy Days. New York: Harper, 1942.

"Introduction." In Charles Péguy, *Basic Verities: Prose and Poetry*. Trans. by Ann and Julian Green. New York: Pantheon Books, 1943.

Si j'étais vous. Paris: Plon, 1947.

Moïra. Paris: Plon, 1950.

Sud. Paris: Plon, 1953.

L'Ennemi. Paris: Plon, 1954.

Le Malfaiteur. Paris: Plon, 1955.

L'Ombre. Paris: Plon, 1956.

Chaque homme dans sa nuit. Paris: Plon, 1960.

Journal (1928-1958). Paris: Plon, 1961.

Partir avant le jour. Paris: Grasset, 1963.

Mille chemins ouverts. Paris: Grasset, 1964.

Terre lointaine. Paris: Grasset, 1966.

Journal II (1949-1966). Paris: Plon, 1969.
L'Autre. Paris: Plon, 1971.
Journal (1966-1972). Paris: Plon, 1972.
Jeunesse. Paris: Plon, 1974.

OTHER SOURCES

Albérès, René-Marill [René Marill]. *Les Hommes traqués*. Paris: La Nouvelle Edition, 1953.

Albrecht, Milton C. "A Study of Julian Green." *Journal of Abnormal and Social Psychology* 41 (April 1946): 169-88.

________. "Psychological Motives in the Fiction of Julian Green." *Journal of Personality* 16 (March 1948): 278-303.

Blanchet, André. *Littérature et le spirituel*. Vol. 2. Paris: Aubier, 1960.

Brodin, Pierre. *Julien Green*. Classiques du XXe siècle. Paris: Ed. Universitaires, 1957.

Burne, Glenn S. *Julian Green*. New York: Twayne, 1972.

Campbell, Joseph. *The Hero with a Thousand Faces*. New York: Pantheon Books, 1949.

Carrel, Janine. *L'Expérience du seuil dans l'oeuvre de Julien Green*. Zurich: Juris Verlag, 1967.

Cluny, Claude Michel. "Eros et Virginie." *La Nouvelle Revue Française* 163 (July 1, 1966): 107-11.

Eck, Marcel. "La Genèse d'une angoisse: essai de psychanalyse de Julien Green." *La Table ronde* 196 (May 1964): 130-44.

Eigeldinger, Marc. *Julien Green et la tentation de l'irréel*. Paris: Aux Portes de France, 1947.

Eliade, Mircéa. *Images et symboles: essais sur le symbolisme magico-religieux*. Paris: Gallimard, 1952.

Fernandez, Dominique. "Comment on devient homosexuel." *La Quinzaine littéraire* 2 (April 1, 1966): 6-7.

Fongaro, Antoine. *L'Existence dans les romans de Julien Green*. Rome: Angelo Signorelli Ed., 1954.

Frye, Northrop. *Anatomy of Criticism*. New York: Atheneum, 1967.

Gorkine Michel. *Julien Green*. Paris: Nouvelles Editions Debresse, 1956.

Guiomar, Michel. "L'Incendie de Mont-Cinère: Préface à une topo-analyse de Julien Green." *La Revue d'esthétique* 20 (1967): 74-87.

Hoy, Peter C. "The Accessible Past." *The Times Literary Supplement* 3472 (September 12, 1968): 1026-27.

________. *Essai de bibliographie des études en langue française consacrées à Julien Green (1923-1967).* Calepins de bibliographie. Paris, 1970.

________. "Images crépusculaires et images eidétiques chez Julien Green." *La Revue des Lettres Modernes* 130—33 (1966): 75-92.

Jaloux, Edmond. "L'Oeil sur les livres." *Les Nouvelles littéraires*, March 24, 1934, p. 3.

Joye, Jean-Claude. *Julien Green et le monde de la fatalité.* Berne: A. Druck, 1964.

Kanters, Robert. *Des Ecrivains et des hommes.* Paris: René Julliard, 1952.

Maritain, Jacques. *Art et scolastique.* 2d ed. Paris: Louis Rouart et fils, 1927.

________. *Creative Intuition in Art and Poetry.* New York: Pantheon Books, 1953.

Moëller, Charles. *Littérature du XXe siècle et christianisme.* Vol. 1. Paris and Tournai: Casterman, 1953.

Mor, Antonio. *Testimone dell'invisibile.* Civiltà litteraria del novecento. Milan: U. Mursia and Co., 1970.

Petit, Jacques. *Julien Green: "l'homme qui venait d'ailleurs."* Paris: Desclée de Brouwer, 1969.

Peyre, Henri. *French Novelists of Today.* 2d ed. New York: Oxford University Press, 1967.

Poulet, Georges. *Etudes sur le temps humain.* Vol. 4: *Mesure de l'instant.* Paris: Plon, 1968.

Prévost, Jean-Laurent. *Julien Green ou l'âme engagée.* Lyon: Emmanuel Vitte, 1960.

Rose, Marilyn Gaddis. "The Production of Julien Green: Microcosm of Mid-Century Writing." *French Review* 34 (December 1960): 164-69.

Rousseau, Guy Noël. *Sur le chemin de Julien Green.* Neuchâtel: Ed. de la Baconnière, 1965.

Rousseaux, André. *Littérature du vingtième siècle.* Vol. 2, 2d ed. Paris: Albin Michel, 1948.

Saint-Jean, Robert de. *Julien Green par lui-même.* Ecrivains de toujours. Paris: Ed. du Seuil, 1967.

Sémolué, Jean. *Julien Green: ou l'obsession du mal.* Paris: Ed. du Centurion, 1964.

Stokes, Samuel. *Julian Green and the Thorn of Puritanism*. New York: King's Crown Press, 1955.

Uitjerwaal, J. *Julien Green, personnalité et création romanesque*. Assen: Van Gorcum and Co., 1968.

"Un Américain à Paris." *Le Monde*, June 4, 1971, p. 18.

Underhill, Evelyn. *Mysticism: A Study in the Nature and Development of Man's Spiritual Consciousness*. 11th ed. London: Methuen and Co., 1926.

Private interview with M. Julien Green in Paris, April 1971.

Index

The works of Julien Green are listed under his name.

About the Author

John M. Dunaway is assistant professor and chairman of the Department of Modern Foreign Languages at Mercer University, Macon, Georgia.